THE COMPLETE INSTANT POT MINI COOKBOOK

THE BEST GUIDE WITH FAST AND TASTY RECIPES FOR YOUR 3-QUART ELECTRIC PRESSURE COOKER.

SUSAN GRAHAM

CONTENTS

CHAPTER 4: BREAKFAST RECIPES

CHAPTER 5: RICE & PASTA RECIPES

CHAPTER 6: SEAFOOD RECIPES

CHAPTER 7: MEAT RECIPES

CHAPTER 8: VEGETARIAN RECIPES

CHAPTER 9: SOUP & STEW

COPYRIGHT

INTRODUCTION

Instant Pots are extremely popular these days and have brought pressure cooking back into fashion. If you have a small family, a lot of the IPs are too large and bulky, but the Minis - which are just 3-quarts - are a perfect size. Keep reading to learn what pressure cooking is exactly, why it's a great cooking method, and how to use an Instant Pot Mini.

CHAPTER 1: INTRODUCING THE INSTANT POT MINI

When you put an airtight seal on a pot of liquid and heat it, the steam cannot escape and pressure builds up inside. This raises the temperature higher than the normal boiling point of 212-degrees. Specifically, it peaks at 250-degrees. This speeds up the cooking process. The first person to really embrace this idea was a mathematician from the 17th-century. He created "the bone digester," a large cooking vessel he wanted to sell to the poor. The high temperatures would allow them to cook even the toughest meat down into nutritious meat jelly. Being too large and prone to explosions, the bone digester never took off, so it wasn't until the 1939 World's Fair that the first stovetop pressure cooker launched.

As the years went by, electric pressure cookers took over as the device of choice. The very first electric pressure cooker was patented in 1991 in China. In 2008, Robert Wang and two friends began working on designs for a new electric cooker, and in 2010, they released the first Instant Pot. Since then, the brand has become the most well-known electric pressure cooker.

Getting to Know Your IP Mini

All Instant Pots, including the 3-quart models, are composed of an electronic base, a stainless steel pot, and a lid fitted with an airtight silicone seal. To use the Instant Pot, you simply follow a recipe and seal the lid by turning it until you hear a chime. Select the cooking program, adjust the time if necessary, and the pressure cooker begins to cook. After time is up, you will either wait for a natural pressure release or manually quick-release the pressure. To do this, you turn the steam release handle, letting the hot steam escape. Once all the steam and pressure is gone, you can open the Instant Pot.

Instant Pot sells many models in a variety of sizes. The mini Instant Pots are three quarts and include the Duo Mini 7-in-1 and the LUX Mini 6-in-1. They're perfect for making enough food for up to three people and as a portable, lighter cooking device you can take on trips.

Buttons

The Mini Duo is essentially seven appliances in one: rice cooker, pressure cooker, slow cooker, steamer, saute, yogurt maker, and warmer. Let's briefly go over the buttons:

Soup/Broth - the "less" mode is good for soup without meat, "normal" is for soup w/ meat, and "more" is good for bone broth

Meat/Stew - the "less" mode gets a soft texture, "normal" is very soft," and "more" is fall-off-the-bone tender

Bean/Chili - the "less" produces least soft, "normal" is soft, and "more" is very sof t

Rice - "less" produces al dente, "normal" is normal-soft, and "more" is very soft

Porridge - "less" for oatmeal, "normal" for white rice porridge, and "more" for porridges with beans/different rices

Steam - "less" for veggies, "normal" for fish/seafood, "more" for meat

Slow Cook - "less" mimics low setting on slow cookers, "normal" mimics medium, and "more" mimics high

Saute - "less" is for simmer, "normal" is pan searing, and "more" is browning or stir-frying

Pressure Level - choose between high or low pressure

Delay Start - choose when to start your meal with the "+" and "-" buttons, which are used for time

"-" and "=" - reduce or increase cook time

Keep Warm - keeps meal warm at a safe, low temperature

Cancel - turns off and resets I P

Yogurt - "less" is for sweet fermented rice desserts, "normal" ferments milk for yogurt, and "more" pasteurizes milk for yogurt

Pressure Cook - basically the "manual" button, it lets you choose time and pressure without a program

The LUX 6-in-1 is basically the same as the DUO Mini, just without the yogurt function. The control pad layout is also a little different and it has an "Egg" function.

Construction and Safety of IP Mini

Both Mini models are made from high-quality stainless steel with no chemical coating, and the pot is dishwasher-safe. Safety features include a pressure regulator, which prevents those scary explosions of the old days, and a safety lid lock, so no one can open the cooker when it's pressurized. This is important if you have young kids around who might wander into the kitchen and want to check on dinner. The cookers are also equipped with automatic temperature control, temperature monitoring to prevent food burning, and automatic shut-down if the cooker gets too hot.

The power on a pressure cooker is measured in PSI, or pounds per square inch. The higher the PSI, the more pressure builds up and the higher the temperature goes. Low pressure on the Instant Pot hits between 5.8-7.2 PSI, while high pressure is 10.2-11.6. This is the standard range for all electric pressure cooker brands.

CHAPTER 2: CLEANING THE INSTANT POT

As with any cooking appliance, keeping your Instant Pot Mini clean is very important. A clean Instant Pot is one that lasts a long time and continues producing great meals every time. Before cleaning, always unplug the IP and let it cool if you just used it. There are four parts you need to concern yourself with: the outside of the pot, the removable inner pot, the exhaust valve, and the gasket/silicone ring.

The outside

Cleaning the outside of the Instant Pot is easy. It can get grimy and dusty, so just dampen a paper towel or rag and wipe it down. A shiny clean Instant Pot is more than just an attractive appliance on your counter; keeping it clean keeps bugs and bacteria at bay.

The inner pot

Made of stainless steel, this pot can be removed and run through the dishwasher. You can also wash it by hand, but be sure to use a soft sponge since abrasive ones will scratch the surface. Regular dish soap and hot water is all you need.

The exhaust valve

Turn over the lid to your IP Mini, and you'll see a little "hat" with holes fitted to the inside. This is the exhaust valve cap, and food can get stuck in it and the valve itself. Pop off the cap (don't twist) and rinse it out well. Clean out the hole to the valve with something sharp and non-breakable, like a needle.

The gasket/silicone ring

The official name of the airtight silicone sealing ring is the gasket, so if you see that written anywhere, it's referring to the ring. This holds on to a lot of odors, so you want to clean it out at least every two to three meals you make. Like the inner pot, it is dishwasher-safe. If you make something with tomato, fish, onion, or a lot of spices, you'll probably want to soak it in a mixture of water, vinegar, and baking soda. Rinse and dry it well. When it starts to get discolored and you can't seem to get rid of the odors, it's time to replace it. You should also replace the ring when it starts to feel loose in the lid.

Other maintenance tips

When storing your IP, keep the lid off the pot. This lets it air out, so odors aren't trapped. It also lets the IP dry out completely if there's any water from cleanup leftover. If you want your IP to last as long as possible, we recommend hand-washing over using the dishwasher. It can be a pain, yes, but it's gentler on the cooker parts.

CHAPTER 3: TIPS FOR SUCCESS

New to pressure cookers and Instant Pots? They are pretty simple to use, but there are some important tips to remember that make cooking as easy and convenient as possible. There are also common issues a lot of IP users come across, so let's go over the solutions.

Tips

1. Where you are above sea level affects cook time.

For every 1,000 feet you are above sea level, add 5 minutes to the cook time given in a standard recipe.

2. Always put at least ½ cup of liquid into the pot before bringing it to pressure.

This is the minimum amount required to generate steam. A lot of recipes will have more liquid if you're making anything with a sauce, a soup, stew, and so on, but no matter what, you need at least ½ cup. Certain ingredients create their own liquid, like tomatoes, so you'll see recipes that don't call for any liquid. If you aren't sure, add ½ cup just to be safe. You can also reduce the liquid later.

3. You'll frequently use the IP like a skillet before bringing a meal to pressure .

This is what the "saute" function is for. You only need a little bit of oil; you aren't deep-frying anything. Always leave the lid off on this function.

4. To leave room for steam and pressure, only fill your cooker ⅔ of the way full.

If it's too full, the food might be undercooked. For foods full of starch, fill the cooker just ½ of the way full. Food like oatmeal, rice, and pasta tend to get really foamy, and if it's too full, that foam gets in the exhaust valve and makes a mess.

5. Remember that steam is hot.

When you're quick-releasing the pressure from the pot, turn your face away from the IP. That escaping steam is very hot. Wear an oven mitt when opening the valve to protect your fingers.

Troubleshooting

Every cooking device has problems once and a while, and the IP Minis are no exception. Here are the most common issues and how to resolve them:

1. Why isn't my Instant Pot coming to pressure?

If your IP won't pressurize, it's almost always because the lid isn't on properly. You want to hear that musical chime when you turn the lid and have the steam release handle in the "sealed" position. If it's open, all the steam is escaping instead of building up inside the pot. If you've been using your IP for a few years without changing the gasket and it won't pressurize, replace the gasket .

There are two other possible reasons, and they both have to do with the food in the pot. If you don't have that minimum ½ cup of liquid, the IP won't pressurize. If you used a thickener in the recipe like cornstarch or flour, the mixture might be too thick. Thickeners are added later.

2. Food and foam are spraying out of the steam release valve!

Your meal is ready and you open the steam release valve, only to have food or foam spray out. This is most likely because the IP is too full. Certain foods tend to get really foamy when they cook - like beans, grains, rice, and oatmeal - so you only want to fill your IP ½ of the way full. Even non-starchy foods need room in the pot, so you should never fill the cooker more than ⅔ of the way full.

Another reason you're experiencing spraying might be because the recipe actually needs a natural pressure release. This is when you just turn off the cooker and leave the steam release handle alone. Steam and pressure escape from other openings in the cooker. The longer the recipe's cook time, the longer a natural pressure release takes.

3. The meal I made is undercooked.

If your food didn't cook all the way through, you're using the wrong cook time or you used too much liquid. You want to measure very carefully when you're using an IP; an extra ¼ cup of liquid or a few minutes can make a big difference. Depending on how underdone things are, you can return the cooker to pressure for 2-5 minutes. If you think that's too much time, just hit "saute" and finish cooking with the lid off. It's always better to have undercooked food than something overcooked.

4. My food overcooked! What do I do to prevent that next time?

The easiest strategy is to reduce the cook time. If you're someone who always adds a few minutes to a recipe "to make sure," you shouldn't do that with an IP. Because the temperatures are so high, even a few minutes can take a piece of meat from perfect to overcooked. If your food is burned, it's most likely because something got stuck to the bottom. Try using a steamer basket next time or the bowl-in-pot method, which is when you mix ingredients in a bowl and set it in the

IP with some water underneath in the pot. You're basically using the pressure cooker as a steamer. Eggs are often cooked this way.

Another reason for burned food might be because the liquid/sauce is too thick. As we mentioned before, thickeners like cornstarch, flour, and more should be added later and not brought to pressure.

CHAPTER 4: BREAKFAST RECIPES

NUTRITIOUS SPROUT SALAD

Time: 15 minutes

Serve: 3

Ingredients:

- 1 lb Brussels sprouts, trimmed and halved
- 1 cup feta cheese, crumbled
- 1/4 cup cashew nuts, chopped
- 2 tbsp pomegranate seeds
- 2 tbsp butter, melted

Directions:

- Pour 1 cup water into the instant pot and place trivet into the pot.
- Place Brussels sprouts on a trivet. Seal pot with lid and select high pressure for 3 minutes.
- Release pressure using quick release method than open the lid.
- Transfer Brussels sprouts in a bowl and drizzle with melted butter.

- Add remaining ingredients and toss well.
- Serve and enjoy.

Nutritional Value (Amount per Serving):

- Calories 379
- Fat 24.8 g
- Carbohydrates 20.2 g
- Sugar 5.9 g
- Protein 14.8 g
- Cholesterol 65 mg

QUICK STEEL CUT OATS

Time: 10 minutes

Serve : 4

Ingredients:

- 1 1/2 cups steel cut oats
- 1/4 cup maple syrup
- 1/2 cup coconut milk
- 3 cups water
- 1 tbsp coconut oil
- 1/8 tsp salt

Directions:

- Set instant pot on sauté mode. When the display reads hot then add coconut oil.
- Once the oil is melted then add oats and cook for 2 minutes. Stir constantly.
- Add water and salt. Stir well.
- Seal pot with lid and select high pressure for 3 minutes.

- Allow to release pressure naturally then open the lid.
- Add coconut milk and maple syrup and stir well to combine.
- Top with your favorite toppings and serve.

Nutritional Value (Amount per Serving):

- Calories 266
- Fat 12.6 g
- Carbohydrates 35.6 g
- Sugar 13 g
- Protein 4.7 g
- Cholesterol 0 mg

CHEESE MUSHROOM OMELET

Time: 15 minutes

Serve: 4

Ingredients:

- 5 eggs, lightly beaten
- 2 tbsp butter
- 1/2 tbsp cheddar cheese
- 1 bell pepper, chopped
- 1 onion, chopped
- 2 tbsp chives, minced
- 1 1/2 cups mushrooms, sliced
- 1/2 cup coconut milk

Directions:

- Add butter into the instant pot and set the pot on sauté mode.
- In a bowl, add eggs and beat until well combined.
- Add remaining ingredients and mix well. Pour egg mixture into the instant pot and cook for 2 minutes.

- Seal pot with lid and select high pressure for 8 minutes.
- Release pressure using quick release method than open the lid.
- Serve hot and enjoy.

Nutritional Value (Amount per Serving):

- Calories 229
- Fat 18.9 g
- Carbohydrates 7.8 g
- Sugar 4.6 g
- Protein 9.4 g
- Cholesterol 221 mg

MINI BREAKFAST FRITTATAS

Time: 15 minutes

Serve: 3

Ingredients:

- 3 eggs
- 1 scallion, chopped
- 1 zucchini, chopped
- 4 tbsp cheddar cheese, shredded
- 2 bacon slices, cooked and crumbled
- 1/4 tsp lemon pepper seasoning
- 1/4 cup almond milk
- Pepper
- Salt

Directions:

- Pour 1 cup water into the instant pot and then place trivet into the pot.
- Add all ingredients into the bowl and whisk well to combine.

- Pour mixture into the silicone molds and place on top of the trivet.
- Seal pot with lid and select high pressure for 5 minutes.
- Release pressure using quick release method than open the lid.
- Serve immediately and enjoy.

Nutritional Value (Amount per Serving):

- Calories 228
- Fat 17.7 g
- Carbohydrates 4.5 g
- Sugar 2.3 g
- Protein 13.9 g
- Cholesterol 188 mg

CREAMY MASHED POTATOES

Time: 15 minutes

Serve: 4

Ingredients:

- 3 potatoes, peeled and cubed
- 1/2 cup milk
- 3 tbsp butter
- 1 cup water
- 2 tbsp parsley, chopped
- 1/4 cup parmesan cheese, grated
- 1/8 tsp ground black pepper
- 1 tsp Himalayan salt

Directions:

- Add potatoes, salt, and 1 cup water into the instant pot. Stir well.
- Seal pot with lid and select high pressure for 3 minutes.
- Release pressure using quick release method than open the lid.

- Drain potatoes well and place in a large bowl.
- Add butter into the potatoes and mash potatoes using the masher until smooth and creamy.
- Add milk and pepper and stir well to combine.
- Garnish with parmesan cheese and parsley.
- Serve and enjoy.

Nutritional Value (Amount per Serving):

- Calories 352
- Fat 18.4 g
- Carbohydrates 26.7 g
- Protein 15.8 g
- Cholesterol 55 mg

WARM QUINOA WITH PEACHES

Time: 15 minutes

Serve: 3

Ingredients:

- 1 cup quinoa, rinsed and drained
- 3/4 cup half and half
- 1/2 tsp vanilla extract
- 1 cup peaches
- 1 tbsp cinnamon
- 1 cup milk
- 1/2 cup water
- 1 tbsp butter

Directions:

- Add butter into the instant pot and set the pot on sauté mode.
- Once butter is melted then add quinoa and stir for 2 minutes.
- Add milk and water and stir well. Add vanilla and cinnamon and stir.

- Seal pot with lid and select high pressure for 4 minutes.
- Release pressure using quick release method than open the lid.
- Stir in half and half and peaches.
- Serve and enjoy.

Nutritional Value (Amount per Serving):

- Calories 389
- Fat 16.1 g
- Carbohydrates 49.6 g
- Sugar 8.6 g
- Protein 13.1 g
- Cholesterol 39 mg

CREAMY ALMOND PORRIDGE

Time: 25 minutes

Serve: 3

Ingredients:

- 1 eggs, lightly beaten
- 1 1/2 tbsp blueberries
- 1/2 cup almond flour
- 2 tsp butter
- 1 tbsp flax meal
- 1 tbsp sugar
- 1 tbsp heavy cream
- 1 cup water

Directions:

- Add butter into the instant pot and set the pot on sauté mode.
- Add water, ground flax meal, almond flour, and salt into the instant pot and stir well and cook for 2-3 minutes.
- Add beaten egg and stir constantly.

- Seal pot with lid and select high pressure for 10 minutes.
- Release pressure using quick release method than open the lid.
- Stir in blueberries and serve.

Nutritional Value (Amount per Serving):

- Calories 195
- Fat 16 g
- Carbohydrates 9.6 g
- Sugar 5.2 g
- Protein 6.5 g
- Cholesterol 68 mg

PUMPKIN BREAKFAST PORRIDGE

Time: 25 minutes

Serve: 2

Ingredients:

- 4 tbsp can pumpkin
- 2 tbsp butter
- 2 tbsp heavy cream
- 1 1/2 tbsp sugar
- 1/4 tsp vanilla extract
- 2 eggs, lightly beaten
- 1 tsp pumpkin pie spice
- 1 cup water
- 2 tbsp flax meal
- 1/4 cup almond flour
- 1/8 tsp salt

Directions:

- Add butter into the instant pot and set the pot on sauté mode.

- Once butter is melted then add almond flour, pumpkin pie spice, water, and flax meal and cook for 2-3 minutes.
- In a bowl, beat eggs until light. Add remaining ingredients into the egg and mix well.
- Transfer egg mixture into the instant pot and cook for 2 minutes.
- Seal pot with lid and select high pressure for 15 minutes.
- Release pressure using quick release method than open the lid.
- Stir well and serve.

Nutritional Value (Amount per Serving):

- Calories 375
- Fat 31.1 g
- Carbohydrates 17.9 g
- Sugar 11 g
- Protein 10.9 g
- Cholesterol 215 mg

CINNAMON PUMPKIN OATS

Time: 20 minutes

Serve: 4

Ingredients:

- 1 cup steel cut oats
- 1/4 tsp cinnamon
- 1 tbsp brown sugar
- 2 tbsp maple syrup
- 1/4 cup pumpkin
- 1 tsp vanilla
- 1 1/4 cups water
- 14 oz can coconut milk
- 1/2 tsp salt

Directions:

- Add oats, vanilla, water, coconut milk, and salt into the instant pot and stir well.
- Seal pot with lid and select high for 10 minutes.

- Release pressure using quick release method than open the lid.
- Add cinnamon, brown sugar, maple syrup, and pumpkin and stir well.
- Serve and enjoy.

Nutritional Value (Amount per Serving):

- Calories 316
- Fat 22.6 g
- Carbohydrates 27 g
- Sugar 9 g
- Protein 4.9 g
- Cholesterol 0 mg

LENTIL RICE PORRIDGE

Time: 30 minutes

Serve: 4

Ingredients:

- 1/2 cup yellow lentils, soaked and rinsed
- 1 cup rice, soaked and rinsed
- 1 1/2 tsp cumin seeds
- 1 bay leaf
- 2 tbsp butter
- 1 tsp turmeric
- 6 cups water
- 1 1/2 tsp salt

Directions:

- Add butter into the instant pot and set the pot on sauté mode.
- Once butter is melted then add cumin seeds and bay leaf and sauté for 30 seconds.
- Add lentils, turmeric, rice, salt, and water. Stir well.

- Seal instant pot with lid and select high pressure for 20 minutes.
- Allow to release pressure naturally for 20 minutes then release using quick release method.
- Stir and serve.

Nutritional Value (Amount per Serving):

- Calories 301
- Fat 6.5 g
- Carbohydrates 50.2 g
- Sugar 0.1 g
- Protein 9.5 g
- Cholesterol 15 mg

ITALIAN FRITTATA

Time: 15 minutes

Serve: 3

Ingredients:

- 3 eggs, lightly beaten
- 1 tbsp basil, chopped
- 1/2 tbsp butter
- 1 cup cherry tomatoes, halved
- 2 tbsp cheddar cheese
- 1 cup feta cheese, crumbled
- 1/2 onion, chopped
- Pepper
- Salt

Directions:

- Add butter into the instant pot and set the pot on sauté mode.
- In a bowl, beat egg until light. Add remaining ingredients into the egg and mix well.

- Transfer egg mixture into the pot and cook for 2 minutes.
- Seal pot with lid and select high pressure for 5 minutes.
- Release pressure using quick release method than open the lid.
- Serve and enjoy.

Nutritional Value (Amount per Serving):

- Calories 249
- Fat 18.6 g
- Carbohydrates 6.5 g
- Sugar 4.8 g
- Protein 14.6 g
- Cholesterol 218 mg

PERFECT SPINACH CHEESE FRITTATA

Time: 30 minutes

Serve: 3

Ingredients:

- 3 eggs
- 3 egg whites
- 2 tbsp milk
- 1 garlic clove, minced
- 1 cup fresh spinach, chopped
- 1 medium tomato, chopped
- 1/2 cup onion, chopped
- 1 cup mozzarella cheese, shredded
- 1 tbsp olive oil
- Pepper
- Salt

Directions:

- Add oil into the instant pot and set the pot on sauté mode.

- Add garlic and onion and sauté for 3-4 minutes.
- In a bowl, whisk together remaining ingredients and pour into the instant pot.
- Seal pot with lid and select high pressure for 15 minutes.
- Release pressure using quick release method than open the lid.
- Serve and enjoy.

Nutritional Value (Amount per Serving):

- Calories 171
- Fat 11.1 g
- Carbohydrates 5.5 g
- Protein 13.1 g
- Cholesterol 170 mg

YUMMY CHOCOLATE OATMEAL

Time: 15 minutes

Serve: 3

Ingredients:

- 1 cup old fashioned oats
- 1/4 cup maple syrup
- 2 1/2 cups water
- 1 tbsp cocoa powder
- 2 tbsp coconut oil
- 1/8 tsp salt

Directions:

- Add all ingredients except maple syrup into the instant pot and stir well.
- Seal pot with lid and select high pressure for 8 minutes.
- Release pressure using quick release method than open the lid.
- Stir in maple syrup and serve.

Nutritional Value (Amount per Serving):

- Calories 359
- Fat 12.8 g
- Carbohydrates 54.4 g
- Sugar 17.1 g
- Protein 7 g
- Cholesterol 0 mg

MILLET APPLE PORRIDGE

Time: 20 minutes

Serve: 3

Ingredients:

- 6 tbsp dry millet
- 1/4 tsp ground ginger
- 1/2 tsp ground cinnamon
- 1 1/2 cups water
- 1 apple, diced
- 1/4 cup rolled oats
- 1/8 tsp salt

Directions:

- Add all ingredients into the instant pot and stir well to combine.
- Seal pot with lid and select high pressure for 10 minutes.
- Allow to release pressure naturally then open the lid.
- Stir well and serve.

Nutritional Value (Amount per Serving):

- Calories 160
- Fat 1.6 g
- Carbohydrates 33.5 g
- Sugar 7.8 g
- Protein 3.9 g
- Cholesterol 0 mg

STRAWBERRY OATMEAL

Time: 25 minutes

Serve: 3

Ingredients:

- 1 cup steel cut oats
- 1 1/2 cup fresh strawberries, sliced
- 4 tbsp chia seeds
- 3 tbsp brown sugar
- 1/4 cup cream
- 4 cups water
- 1 tbsp butter
- 1/4 tsp salt

Directions:

- Add butter into the instant pot and set the pot on sauté mode.
- Once butter is melted then add oats and stir constantly for 3 minutes.
- Add water, brown sugar, cream, and salt. Stir well.

- Seal pot with lid and select high pressure for 10 minutes.
- Allow to release pressure naturally then open the lid.
- Add chia seeds and strawberries. Stir well.
- Serve and enjoy.

Nutritional Value (Amount per Serving):

- Calories 246
- Fat 10.3 g
- Carbohydrates 37.4 g
- Sugar 12.9 g
- Protein 6.3 g
- Cholesterol 14 mg

SWEET QUINOA PORRIDGE

Time: 20 minutes

Serve: 3

Ingredients:

- 1 cup quinoa, rinsed
- 1 tsp vanilla extract
- 1 tbsp coconut oil
- 3 tbsp maple syrup
- 1 cup coconut milk
- 1 cup water

Directions:

- Add all ingredients into the instant pot and stir well to combine.
- Seal pressure cooker with lid and select high pressure for 2 minutes.
- Allow to release pressure naturally for 10 minutes then release using quick release method.

- Stir well and serve with your choice of topping.

Nutritional Value (Amount per Serving):

- Calories 488
- Fat 27.1 g
- Carbohydrates 54.4 g
- Sugar 14.8 g
- Protein 9.8 g
- Cholesterol 0 mg

YUMMY RICE PUDDING

Time: 20 minutes

Serve: 3

Ingredients:

- 3/4 cup jasmine rice, rinsed and drained
- 1 cup coconut milk
- 1/2 cup sugar
- 1/4 tsp ground cardamom
- 3 cups milk
- 1/8 tsp salt

Directions:

- Add rice, milk, sugar, and salt into the instant pot and stir everything well.
- Seal pot with lid and select high pressure for 15 minutes.
- Allow to release pressure naturally then open the lid.
- Add cardamom and coconut milk and stir well.
- Serve warm and enjoy.

Nutritional Value (Amount per Serving):

- Calories 592
- Fat 24.1 g
- Carbohydrates 85.9 g
- Sugar 47 g
- Protein 12.9 g
- Cholesterol 20 mg

QUINOA PILAF

Time: 30 minutes

Serve: 3

Ingredients:

- 1 cup quinoa, rinsed and drained
- 1/2 tbsp parsley, chopped
- 1/2 tsp garlic powder
- 1 cup chicken broth
- 1 tsp garlic, minced
- 1 tbsp onion, minced
- 1 tbsp celery, minced
- 1 1/2 tbsp butter
- 1/8 tsp black pepper
- 1/2 tsp kosher salt

Directions:

- Add 1 tbsp butter into the instant pot and set the pot on sauté mode.

- Once butter is melted then add celery, quinoa, garlic, and onion and cook for 5 minutes. Stir every minute.
- Add remaining butter, paprika, pepper, garlic powder, broth, and salt. Stir well.
- Seal pot with lid and select high pressure for 1 minute.
- Allow to release pressure naturally then open the lid.
- Add parsley and stir well. Fluff quinoa with fork and serve.

Nutritional Value (Amount per Serving):

- Calories 278
- Fat 9.7 g
- Carbohydrates 37.8 g
- Sugar 0.5 g
- Protein 9.9 g
- Cholesterol 15 mg

SWEET POTATO OATS

Time: 25 minutes

Serve: 2

Ingredients:

- 1/2 cup steel cut oats
- 1/4 cup almond milk
- 1/8 tsp ginger
- 1/4 tsp cardamom
- 1/2 tsp cinnamon
- 1/2 tsp vanilla extract
- 1 1/3 cup water
- 2 tbsp raisins
- 1 cup sweet potato, chopped
- Pinch of salt

Directions:

- Add oats, spices, water, raisins, and sweet potato into the instant pot and stir well.

- Seal pot with lid and select low pressure and set the timer for 15 minutes.
- Release pressure using quick release method than open the lid.
- Add sweet potato chunks and stir to blend.
- Add a pinch of salt and almond milk and stir well.
- Serve and enjoy.

Nutritional Value (Amount per Serving):

- Calories 270
- Fat 8.7 g
- Carbohydrates 44.2 g
- Sugar 13.2 g
- Protein 5.7 g
- Cholesterol 0 mg

CHAPTER 5: RICE & PASTA RECIPES

JERK CHICKEN & RICE

Time: 20 minutes

Serve: 2

Ingredients:

- 2 chicken thighs, skinless and boneless
- 1 cup chicken broth
- 1 tbsp jerk seasoning
- 1 garlic clove, minced
- 1/2 small onion, diced
- 3/4 cup long grain rice, rinsed
- 2 tsp olive oil

Directions:

- Set instant pot on sauté mode. When instant pot display reads hot then add olive oil.
- Add onion and sauté for few minutes or until onion softens.
- Add garlic and sauté for 20 seconds. Stir constantly.
- Add jerk seasoning and stir well to mix.

- Add rice and chicken broth and stir well. Now add the chicken.
- Seal instant pot with lid and select pressure cook mode and set the timer for 7 minutes.
- Allow to release pressure naturally for 5 minutes then release using quick release method than open the lid.
- Stir well and serve.

Nutritional Value (Amount per Serving):

- Calories 599
- Fat 16.7 g
- Carbohydrates 58.1 g
- Sugar 1.2 g
- Protein 49.9 g
- Cholesterol 130 mg

TASTY CREAM CHEESE RISOTTO

Time: 20 minutes

Serve: 4

Ingredients:

- 2 1/2 cups Arborio rice
- 6 oz cream cheese, softened
- 1/2 cup pecans, chopped
- 1 tbsp pepper
- 2 tbsp fresh lemon juice
- 1 cup white wine
- 5 cups chicken broth
- 2 tbsp garlic, minced
- 2 onions, chopped
- 4 tbsp olive oil

Directions:

- Add olive oil into the instant pot and set the pot on sauté mode.

- When the display reads hot then add onions and garlic and sauté for 3 minutes.
- Stir in wine and rice and cook until wine absorbed.
- Add broth and stir well. Seal pot with lid and select high pressure for 6 minutes.
- Allow to release pressure naturally then open the lid.
- Season with pepper and lemon juice and stir in cream cheese.
- Garnish with chopped pecans and serve.

Nutritional Value (Amount per Serving):

- Calories 566
- Fat 18.1 g
- Carbohydrates 78.4 g
- Sugar 4.6 g
- Protein 15.1 g
- Cholesterol 5 mg

EASY COCONUT RICE

Time: 20 minutes

Serve: 4

Ingredients:

- 2 cups rice, soaked and drained
- 1/2 cup fresh coriander leaves, chopped
- 1 cup unsweetened coconut, grated
- 1 tbsp cinnamon powder
- 1/4 tbsp cloves
- 1/2 cup currants
- 4 tbsp olive oil
- 4 cups vegetable stock
- 1 tbsp salt

Directions:

- Add olive oil into the instant pot and set the pot on sauté mode.

- Add cloves and cinnamon powder into the pot and sauté for 30 seconds.
- Add rice and stir well. Add remaining ingredients and cook for 1 minute.
- Seal pot with lid and cook on high for 6 minutes.
- Allow to release pressure naturally then open the lid.
- Stir well and serve.

Nutritional Value (Amount per Serving):

- Calories 538
- Fat 21.4 g
- Carbohydrates 79.2 g
- Sugar 2.4 g
- Protein 7.5 g
- Cholesterol 0 mg

CHICKEN CHEESE PASTA

Time: 20 minutes

Serve: 4

Ingredients:

- 1 lb chicken breasts, skinless, boneless, and cut into chunks
- 2 tbsp parmesan cheese
- 1 1/2 cups cheddar cheese, shredded
- 1/2 tbsp mustard
- 1 cup hot water
- 3/4 cup heavy cream
- 8 oz pasta
- 2 tbsp butter
- 1/2 tbsp olive oil
- 1/4 tsp pepper
- 1/2 tsp sea salt

Directions:

- Add olive oil into the instant pot and set the pot on sauté mode.
- When instant pot display reads hot then add chicken chunks and sauté for 4-5 minutes.
- Add remaining ingredients except for cheeses and heavy cream. Stir well.
- Seal pot with lid and select high pressure for 12 minutes.
- Allow to release pressure naturally then open the lid.
- Now set the pot on sauté mode and add cheddar cheese, parmesan cheese, and heavy cream. Stir well until cheese is melted.
- Serve and enjoy.

Nutritional Value (Amount per Serving):

- Calories 650
- Fat 35.6 g
- Carbohydrates 33.3 g
- Sugar 0.1 g
- Protein 47.1 g
- Cholesterol 220 mg

TASTY CHEESEBURGER MACARONI

Time: 20 minutes

Serve: 3

Ingredients:

- 1/2 lb ground beef
- 1 cup elbow macaroni, uncooked
- 1/2 tsp basil
- 1/2 onion, chopped
- 1 1/2 cups chicken broth
- 1/2 cup cheddar cheese, shredded
- 1 tbsp Italian seasoning
- 14 oz can tomatoes, diced
- 7.5 oz can tomato sauce
- 1 1/2 tsp garlic, minced
- 1/2 tbsp seasoning salt

Directions:

- Set instant pot on sauté mode.

- When instant pot display reads hot then add onion and ground beef and sauté until meat is no longer pink.
- Add garlic, seasoning salt, Italian seasoning, and basil and sauté for 5 minutes.
- Add tomatoes, tomato sauce, and broth and stir well.
- Add macaroni in and stir well. Seal pot with lid and select high pressure for 4 minutes.
- Release pressure using quick release method than open the lid.
- Stir in cheese and serve.

Nutritional Value (Amount per Serving):

- Calories 408
- Fat 13.6 g
- Carbohydrates 34.9 g
- Sugar 9.9 g
- Protein 36.1 g
- Cholesterol 91 mg

QUICK CHEESE MACARONI

Time: 10 minutes

Serve: 3

Ingredients:

- 1/2 lb pasta
- 6 oz evaporated milk
- 1/2 cup mozzarella cheese, grated
- 1/2 cup cheddar cheese, shredded
- 16 oz chicken broth
- Pepper
- Salt

Directions:

- Add broth and pasta into the instant pot. Seal pot with lid and select high pressure for 5 minutes.
- Release pressure using quick release method than open the lid.
- Add milk and cheese and stir until pasta is coated. Season with pepper and salt.

- Serve and enjoy.

Nutritional Value (Amount per Serving):

- Calories 407
- Fat 14 g
- Carbohydrates 48.1 g
- Sugar 6.2 g
- Protein 21.5 g
- Cholesterol 94 mg

DELICIOUS CREAMY ZITI

Time: 20 minutes

Serve: 4

Ingredients:

- 1/2 cup mozzarella cheese, shredded
- 1 cup parmesan cheese, shredded
- 1 cup pasta sauce
- 8 oz ziti pasta
- 1 tsp garlic, minced
- 1 cup heavy cream
- 1 1/2 cups chicken broth
- Pepper
- Salt

Directions:

- Add chicken broth, heavy cream, garlic, pepper, salt, and noodles to the instant pot.
- Seal pot with lid and select high pressure for 6 minutes.

- Allow to release pressure naturally then open the lid.
- Add pasta sauce and stir well. Slowly add cheese and stir until cheese melt and sauce thicken.
- Serve and enjoy.

Nutritional Value (Amount per Serving):

- Calories 430
- Fat 20.7 g
- Carbohydrates 41.9 g
- Sugar 5.8 g
- Protein 18.6 g
- Cholesterol 100 mg

CHICKEN FLORENTINE

Time: 20 minutes

Serve: 4

Ingredients:

- 3 cups baby spinach
- 1 cup parmesan cheese, shredded
- 1 chicken breast, cut into chunks
- 8 oz linguine noodles, break in half
- 1 tsp garlic, minced
- 1 1/2 cups heavy cream
- 2 cups chicken broth
- Pepper
- Salt

Directions:

- Add broth, garlic, heavy cream, pepper, and salt into the instant pot and stir well.
- Add chicken and stir well. Add noodles and stir well to coat.

- Seal pot with lid and select high pressure for 6 minutes.
- Allow to release pressure naturally for 6 minutes then release using quick release method.
- Add parmesan cheese and stir until cheese melt.
- Now add spinach stir for a minute.
- Serve and enjoy.

Nutritional Value (Amount per Serving):

- Calories 661
- Fat 24.9 g
- Carbohydrates 86.8 g
- Sugar 4.5 g
- Protein 25.6 g
- Cholesterol 76 mg

PERFECT ALFREDO

Time: 20 minutes

Serve: 4

Ingredients:

- 1/2 lb dry linguine noodles, break in half
- 3/4 cup parmesan cheese, shredded
- 1 tsp garlic, minced
- 1 1/2 cups heavy cream
- 1 1/2 cups vegetable broth
- Pepper
- Salt

Directions:

- Add vegetable broth, heavy cream, garlic, pepper, salt, and noodles to the instant pot.
- Seal pot with lid and select high pressure for 6 minutes.
- Release pressure using quick release method than open the lid.
- Add parmesan cheese and stir until cheese melted.

- Serve and enjoy.

Nutritional Value (Amount per Serving):

- Calories 279
- Fat 22.8 g
- Carbohydrates 7.7 g
- Sugar 0.6 g
- Protein 11.2 g
- Cholesterol 76 mg

SIMPLE TOMATO RICE

Time: 25 minutes

Serve: 3

Ingredients:

- 1 cup rice, soaked and drained
- 3 tbsp olive oil
- 1 cup water
- 1 tbsp cumin seeds
- 8 tomatoes, sliced
- 1/2 tsp pepper
- 1/2 tbsp salt

Directions:

- Add olive oil into the instant pot and set the pot on sauté mode.
- When instant pot display reads hot then add cumin seeds and sauté for 30 seconds.

- Add tomatoes and sauté for 6 minutes. Add rice, pepper, and salt and stir well.
- Seal pot with lid and select high pressure for 6 minutes.
- Allow to release pressure naturally then open the lid.
- Stir well and serve.

Nutritional Value (Amount per Serving):

- Calories 413
- Fat 15.5 g
- Carbohydrates 63.2 g
- Sugar 8.8 g
- Protein 7.7 g
- Cholesterol 0 mg

MUSHROOM PEA RISOTTO

Time: 30 minutes

Serve: 3

Ingredients:

- 1/2 cup Arborio rice
- 2 tbsp parmesan cheese, grated
- 1/4 cup frozen peas, thawed
- 1 cup baby spinach
- 1/8 tsp dried thyme
- 1 cup chicken broth
- 4 oz cremini mushrooms, sliced
- 1/2 onion, diced
- 1 garlic clove, minced
- 2 tbsp butter
- Pepper
- Salt

Directions:

- Add 1 tablespoon of butter into the instant pot and set the pot on sauté mode.
- Once butter is melted then add onion and garlic and sauté for 2-3 minutes.
- Add mushrooms and cook until tender, about 3-4 minutes. Season with pepper and salt.
- Add broth, thyme, and rice and stir well. Seal pot with lid and select high pressure for 6 minutes.
- Release pressure using quick release method than open the lid.
- Add spinach and remaining butter and stir until spinach is wilted about 2 minutes.
- Stir in parmesan cheese and peas, about 1 minute.
- Serve hot and enjoy.

Nutritional Value (Amount per Serving):

- Calories 239
- Fat 9.3 g
- Carbohydrates 31.4 g
- Sugar 2.3 g
- Protein 7.3 g
- Cholesterol 23 mg

VEGETABLE PARMESAN RISOTTO

Time: 25 minutes

Serve: 4

Ingredients:

- 1 1/2 cups Arborio rice
- 1 tbsp butter
- 1/2 lemon juice
- 1 tbsp parsley, chopped
- 1/2 onion, chopped
- 3 garlic cloves, minced
- 1/2 cup dry white wine
- 3 1/2 cups chicken broth
- 5 asparagus, sliced
- 1 cup fresh spinach
- 2 tsp olive oil
- 1/2 cup parmesan cheese, shredded
- 1 lb shrimp, peeled and deveined
- Pepper
- Salt

Directions:

- Add 1 tsp olive oil into the instant pot and set the pot on sauté mode.
- Add asparagus and cook for 2-3 minutes or until softened.
- Remove asparagus from pot and set aside. Add garlic and onion and sauté for a minute.
- Add butter and melt. Add rice and stir for 1-2 minutes.
- Add white wine and stir well.
- Add broth and parmesan. Stir. Season with pepper and salt.
- Seal pot with lid and select high pressure for 8 minutes.
- Release pressure using quick release method than open the lid.
- Set instant pot on sauté mode. Move risotto to one side of the pot.
- Now add remaining oil to other side then add veggies and shrimp. Cook shrimp for 3-4 minutes or until shrimp are pink.
- Add spinach and cook until wilted. Stir everything well in the pot.
- Drizzle with lemon juice and sprinkle with chopped parsley.
- Serve and enjoy.

Nutritional Value (Amount per Serving):

- Calories 551
- Fat 11.5 g
- Carbohydrates 63.3 g
- Sugar 1.8 g
- Protein 39.5 g
- Cholesterol 254 mg

PARMESAN SHRIMP RISOTTO

Time: 30 minutes

Serve: 4

Ingredients:

- 1 lb shrimp, peeled, deveined, and chopped
- 1/2 cup parmesan cheese, grated
- 1 cup clam juice
- 3 cups chicken broth
- 1/4 cup dry sherry
- 1 1/2 cups Arborio rice
- 1 tbsp paprika
- 1 tbsp oregano leaves, minced
- 1 roasted red pepper, chopped
- 1 onion, chopped
- 2 tbsp butter
- 1/2 tsp black pepper
- 1/2 tsp salt

Directions:

- Add butter into the instant pot and set pot on sauté mode.
- Once butter is melted then add onion and roasted pepper and cook for 4 minutes.
- Stir in the oregano, pepper, paprika, and salt and cook for a minute.
- Add rice and stir for a minute. Add sherry and cook until absorbed.
- Add clam juice and broth. Stir. Seal pot with lid and select high pressure for 10 minutes.
- Release pressure using quick release method than open the lid.
- Set pot on sauté mode and add shrimp and stir until shrimp is cooked about 2 minutes.
- Serve and enjoy.

Nutritional Value (Amount per Serving):

- Calories 600
- Fat 14.1 g
- Carbohydrates 71.2 g
- Sugar 4.7 g
- Protein 41.5 g
- Cholesterol 269 mg

BASIL TOMATO RISOTTO

Time: 20 minutes

Serve: 4

Ingredients:

- 1 1/2 cups Arborio rice
- 1 tbsp dried basil
- 1 cup cherry tomatoes, cut in half
- 3 tbsp basil pesto
- 2 cups vegetable stock
- 1 onion, diced
- 1 tbsp butter
- 1 tbsp olive oil
- 1/2 tsp salt

Directions:

- Add butter and oil into the instant pot and set the pot on sauté mode.

- Add onion and sauté until softened. Add Arborio rice and cook for 3-5 minutes.
- Add stock, pesto, and salt. Stir well.
- Seal pot with lid and select high pressure for 5 minutes.
- Release pressure using quick release method than open the lid.
- Add tomatoes, parmesan, and basil and stir until well combined.
- Serve and enjoy.

Nutritional Value (Amount per Serving):

- Calories 356
- Fat 9.6 g
- Carbohydrates 62.7 g
- Protein 5.7 g
- Cholesterol 8 mg

HEALTHY VEGGIE PASTA

Time: 20 minutes

Serve: 3

Ingredients:

- 1 cup vegetable stock
- 1/2 bell pepper, chopped
- 1 cup spinach, chopped
- 1/2 tomato, diced
- 1/2 medium yellow squash, chopped
- 1/2 small onion, diced
- 12 oz pasta sauce
- 6 oz spiral pasta

Directions:

- Add vegetables, pasta sauce, and stock and stir well.
- Seal pot with lid and select high pressure for 4 minutes.
- Allow to release pressure naturally then open the lid.
- Stir well and serve.

Nutritional Value (Amount per Serving):

- Calories 325
- Fat 4.9 g
- Carbohydrates 62.2 g
- Sugar 13.1 g
- Protein 11.2 g
- Cholesterol 2 mg

SQUASH LEMON RISOTTO

Time: 30 minutes

Serve: 3

Ingredients:

- 3/4 cup Arborio rice
- 1/4 cup parmesan cheese, grated
- 1 tbsp parsley, chopped
- 1 tbsp lemon juice
- 2 cups chicken stock
- 1/2 cup dry white wine
- 1/2 tbsp garlic, minced
- 1/2 lb summer squash, diced
- 1/4 cup onion, diced
- 1 tbsp olive oil
- 1/4 tsp pepper
- 1/2 tsp salt

Directions:

- Add oil into the instant pot and set the pot on sauté mode.
- When instant pot display reads hot then add onions and sauté for 3-4 minutes.
- Add squash, pepper, garlic, and salt and cook for 2 minutes.
- Add rice and cook for 1-2 minutes. Stir frequently.
- Add wine and stir well and cook for 2 minutes.
- Add stock and stir. Seal pot with lid and select high pressure for 4 minutes.
- Release pressure using quick release method than open the lid.
- Add parmesan, parsley, and lemon juice. Mix well.
- Serve and enjoy.

Nutritional Value (Amount per Serving):

- Calories 297
- Fat 8.6 g
- Carbohydrates 42.9 g
- Sugar 3.7 g
- Protein 8.7 g
- Cholesterol 10 mg

ITALIAN PORK RISOTTO

Time: 40 minutes

Serve: 3

Ingredients:

- 1 cup Arborio rice, soaked and drained
- 1 1/2 cups chicken broth
- 1/4 cup parmesan cheese
- 1/2 cup water
- 1 tbsp lemon juice
- 1 tbsp garlic, minced
- 1 onion, chopped
- 4 pork chops
- 1 1/2 tbsp olive oil

Directions:

- Add olive oil into the instant pot and set the pot on sauté mode.

- When instant pot display reads hot then add pork chops and cook until browned.
- Add garlic and onion and sauté for 2 minutes.
- Add rice and stir well to coat. Add water and lemon juice. Stir.
- Seal pot with lid and select high pressure for 20 minutes.
- Allow to release pressure naturally then open the lid.
- Add cheese and stir well.
- Serve and enjoy.

Nutritional Value (Amount per Serving):

- Calories 779
- Fat 41.9 g
- Carbohydrates 56.2 g
- Sugar 2 g
- Protein 41.3 g
- Cholesterol 111 mg

CREAMY VEGETABLE PASTA

Time: 15 minutes

Serve: 3

Ingredients:

- 16 oz ziti pasta
- 2 cups vegetable broth
- 1 cup white wine
- 3 garlic cloves, minced
- 1 cup frozen peas
- 2 cups zucchini, chopped
- 1 cup heavy cream
- 1 cup mozzarella cheese

Directions:

- Add pasta, garlic, vegetables, broth, and white wine into the instant pot and stir well.
- Seal pot with lid and select high pressure for 4 minutes.
- Release pressure using quick release method than open the lid.

- Set pot on sauté mode. Add heavy cream and cheese and stir until cheese is melted or sauce thickens.
- Serve and enjoy.

Nutritional Value (Amount per Serving):

- Calories 749
- Fat 21.2 g
- Carbohydrates 98.1 g
- Sugar 4.9 g
- Protein 27.7 g
- Cholesterol 170 mg

DELICIOUS PARMESAN PASTA

Time: 15 minutes

Serve: 3

Ingredients:

- 8 oz pasta
- 2 tbsp parsley, chopped
- 4 oz parmesan cheese, grated
- 1/2 cup water
- 1/2 cup heavy cream
- 1/2 cup chicken broth
- 1 garlic clove, minced
- 1 tbsp butter

Directions:

- Add butter into the instant pot and set the pot on sauté mode.
- Once butter is melted then add garlic and stir for 30 seconds.
- Add pasta, water, heavy cream and broth. Stir well.
- Seal pot with lid and select high pressure for 3 minutes.

- Release pressure using quick release method than open the lid.
- Add cheese and stir until cheese is melted.
- Garnish with parsley and serve.

Nutritional Value (Amount per Serving):

- Calories 451
- Fat 21.3 g
- Carbohydrates 43.9 g
- Sugar 0.2 g
- Protein 22.1 g
- Cholesterol 120 mg

TENDER AND CREAMY CHICKEN RIGGIES

Time: 15 minutes

Serve: 3

Ingredients:

- 2 cups water
- 1/2 tbsp olive oil
- 2 oz Romano cheese
- 4 oz mushrooms, sliced
- 14 oz alfredo sauce
- 14 oz marinara sauce
- 8 oz rigatoni
- 1/2 lb chicken breast, cubed
- 1 hot cherry peppers, chopped
- 1 1/2 sweet peppers, chopped
- 1/2 tsp red pepper flakes
- 1/2 tsp parsley
- 1/2 tsp onion powder
- 1/2 tsp garlic powder
- 1/2 tsp black pepper

- 1/2 tsp salt

Directions:

- Add oil into the instant pot and set the pot on sauté mode.
- Add chicken and spices and sauté for 2-3 minutes.
- Add water, vegetables, marinara sauce, and pasta and stir well.
- Seal pot with lid and select high pressure for 5 minutes.
- Release pressure using quick release method than open the lid.
- Add Romano cheese and alfredo sauce and stir well.
- Serve and enjoy.

Nutritional Value (Amount per Serving):

- Calories 632
- Fat 35.8 g
- Carbohydrates 40.3 g
- Sugar 9.2 g
- Protein 36.9 g
- Cholesterol 131 mg

SPICY BROWN RICE

Time: 25 minutes

Serve: 3

Ingredients:

- 1 cup brown rice, uncooked
- 1/2 tbsp cumin
- 1/4 tsp onion powder
- 1 tbsp tomato paste
- 1 cup water
- 1 tbsp chili powder
- 1/4 tsp garlic powder
- 1/2 tsp salt

Directions:

- Add water and rice into the instant pot.
- Seal pot with lid and select high pressure for 20 minutes.
- Release pressure using quick release method than open the lid.
- Add remaining ingredients and stir well.

- Serve and enjoy.

Nutritional Value (Amount per Serving):

- Calories 247
- Fat 2.4 g
- Carbohydrates 51.4 g
- Sugar 1 g
- Protein 5.5 g
- Cholesterol 0 mg

CORN RISOTTO

Time: 25 minutes

Serve: 4

Ingredients:

- 1 cup Arborio rice
- 1 onion, chopped
- 1 tsp mix herbs
- 3 cups chicken stock
- 1 tbsp olive oil
- 1/2 cup sweet corn
- 1/2 cup peas
- 1 red pepper, diced
- 2 garlic cloves, minced
- 1/4 pepper
- 1/2 tsp salt

Directions:

- Add olive oil in instant pot and set the pot on sauté mode.

- Add onion and garlic and sauté for 4 minutes.
- Add rice and stir well. Add remaining ingredients and stir well.
- Seal pot with lid and select high pressure for 8 minutes.
- Release pressure using quick release method than open the lid.
- Serve and enjoy.

Nutritional Value (Amount per Serving):

- Calories 262
- Fat 4.6 g
- Carbohydrates 49.9 g
- Protein 6 g
- Cholesterol 0 mg

FLAVORFUL SPAGHETTI

Time: 25 minutes

Serve: 2

Ingredients:

- 6 oz spaghetti noodles
- 2 tbsp parmesan cheese
- 1 1/4 cups chicken stock
- 2 tbsp tomato paste
- 1 cup jar spaghetti sauce
- 1/2 tsp dried oregano
- 1/2 tsp dried basil
- 1 garlic clove, minced
- 1/2 onion, diced
- 1/2 lb ground beef
- 1 tbsp olive oil
- 1/2 tsp salt

Directions:

- Set instant pot on sauté mode and olive oil into the pot.
- Add ground beef and sauté for 3 minutes, stir and break meat with a spoon.
- Add onion and cook for 4 minutes.
- Stir in garlic, oregano, basil, spaghetti sauce, chicken stock, tomato paste, parmesan cheese, pepper, and salt. Stir well.
- Turn off the pot. Break noodles in half and add layer them in the meat mixture.
- Seal instant pot with lid and select pressure cook mode and set the timer for 8 minutes.
- Once the timer goes off then release pressure using quick release method than open the lid.
- Stir well to combine.
- Serve and enjoy.

Nutritional Value (Amount per Serving):

- Calories 594
- Fat 18.4 g
- Carbohydrates 57.9 g
- Sugar 6 g
- Protein 48.1 g
- Cholesterol 167 mg

WALNUT CHEESE RISOTTO

Time: 25 minutes

Serve: 4

Ingredients:

- 2 1/2 cups Arborio rice
- 4 oz cream cheese, softened
- 5 cups chicken stock
- 1 tbsp pepper
- 1 cup white wine
- 1/4 cup blue cheese, crumbled
- 1/2 cups walnuts, chopped
- 1 1/2 cups parmesan cheese
- 3 tbsp fresh lemon juice
- 2 onions, chopped
- 2 tbsp garlic, minced
- 4 tbsp olive oil

Directions:

- Add olive oil into the instant pot and set pot on sauté mode.
- Add onion and garlic and sauté for 3 minutes.
- Add rice, broth, and wine and stir well. Seal pot with lid and select high pressure for 6 minutes.
- Allow to release pressure naturally then open the lid.
- Season with pepper and lemon juice. Stir all the cheese except parmesan cheese.
- Garnish with parmesan cheese and walnuts.
- Serve and enjoy.

Nutritional Value (Amount per Serving):

- Calories 578
- Fat 41.4 g
- Carbohydrates 22.7 g
- Sugar 5.1 g
- Protein 22.5 g
- Cholesterol 49 mg

CAJUN RICE

Time: 25 minutes

Serve: 4

Ingredients:

- 1 cup long grain rice, rinsed and drained
- 2 tsp hot sauce
- 1 tsp dried oregano
- 2 bay leaves
- 1 cup water
- 1 tbsp Cajun seasoning
- 1 lb ground beef
- 1/2 cup onion, diced
- 1/2 cup bell pepper, diced
- 1/2 cup celery, diced
- 2 tbsp olive oil
- 1 tsp salt

Directions:

- Add oil into the instant pot and set the pot on sauté mode.
- When instant pot display reads hot then add ground beef and cook until beef is browned.
- Add bay leaf, rice, hot sauce, Cajun seasoning, and salt and stir to combine.
- Add broth and stir well. Seal pot with lid and cook on high pressure for 4 minutes.
- Allow to release pressure naturally then open the lid.
- Stir and serve.

Nutritional Value (Amount per Serving):

- Calories 453
- Fat 14.5 g
- Carbohydrates 40.1 g
- Sugar 1.6 g
- Protein 38.2 g
- Cholesterol 101 mg

EASY HERBED RICE

Time: 35 minutes

Serve: 4

Ingredients:

- 1 cup long grain rice, rinsed and drained
- 1 tbsp butter
- 1 1/2 cups vegetable stock
- 1/4 cup cilantro, chopped
- 1 tbsp parsley, chopped
- 1 tbsp chives, chopped
- 1 tbsp dill, chopped
- 1 tsp salt

Directions:

- Add all ingredients into the instant pot and stir well to combine.
- Seal pot with lid and select high pressure for 4 minutes.
- Allow to release pressure naturally then open the lid.

- Stir well and serve.

Nutritional Value (Amount per Serving):

- Calories 200
- Fat 3.8 g
- Carbohydrates 38.1 g
- Sugar 0.6 g
- Protein 3.6 g
- Cholesterol 8 mg

SIMPLE ZUCCHINI NOODLES

Time: 15 minutes

Serve: 2

Ingredients:

- 1/2 lb zucchini, spiralized
- 2 tbsp parmesan cheese, grated
- 1/2 tbsp sour cream
- 1/4 cup cream cheese
- 2 tbsp butter
- Pepper
- Salt

Directions:

- In a bowl, mix together sour cream, parmesan cheese, and cream cheese.
- Add butter into the instant pot and set the pot on sauté mode.
- Once butter is melted then add zucchini noodles and stir well.
- Seal pot with lid and select high pressure for 5 minutes.

- Allow to release pressure naturally then open the lid.
- Top with sour cream mixture and stir to combine. Season with pepper and salt.
- Serve and enjoy.

Nutritional Value (Amount per Serving):

- Calories 246
- Fat 23.6 g
- Carbohydrates 4.7 g
- Sugar 2 g
- Protein 5.3 g
- Cholesterol 68 mg

YUMMY MAC & CHEESE

Time: 15 minutes

Serve: 4

Ingredients:

- 8 oz elbow macaroni
- 2/3 cup heavy cream
- 1 cup cheddar cheese, shredded
- 2 tbsp butter
- 2 cups chicken stock
- 1/4 tsp pepper
- 1/4 tsp salt

Directions:

- Set instant pot on sauté mode and pour chicken stock into the instant pot.
- Add butter, pepper, and salt. Stir well and bring to simmer.
- Add macaroni and stir well. Seal instant pot with lid and select

pressure cook mode and set it on high then set the timer for 4 minutes.

- Once the timer goes off then release pressure using quick release method than open the lid carefully.
- Add shredded cheese and stir well and let it melt.
- Stir in heavy cream and season with salt as per your taste.
- Serve and enjoy.

Nutritional Value (Amount per Serving):

- Calories 449
- Fat 23.7 g
- Carbohydrates 43.7 g
- Sugar 2 g
- Protein 15.2 g
- Cholesterol 72 mg

CHAPTER 6: SEAFOOD RECIPES

DELIGHTFUL SALMON DINNER

Time: 15 minutes

Serve: 3

Ingredients:

- 1 lb salmon fillet, cut into three pieces
- 1 tsp ground cumin
- 1 tsp red chili powder
- 1 garlic clove, minced
- Pepper
- Salt

Directions:

- Pour 1 1/2 cups water into the instant pot and place trivet into the pot.
- In a small bowl, mix together all ingredients except salmon.
- Rub salmon pieces with spice mixture and place on top of the trivet.

- Seal pot with lid and select steam mode and set the timer for 2 minutes.
- Release pressure using quick release method than open the lid.
- Serve hot and enjoy.

Nutritional Value (Amount per Serving):

- Calories 207
- Fat 9.7 g
- Carbohydrates 1.1 g
- Sugar 0.1 g
- Protein 29.6 g
- Cholesterol 67 mg

BEST STEAMED CLAMS

Time: 15 minutes

Serve: 3

Ingredients:

- 1 lb mushy shell clams
- 1 tsp garlic powder
- 1/4 cup lemon juice
- 2 tbsp butter, melted
- 1/4 cup white wine

Directions:

- In a bowl, mix together white wine, lemon juice, garlic powder, and butter and set aside.
- Place trivet into the instant pot then add white wine mixture to the pot.
- Arrange clams on the trivet. Seal pot with lid and select high pressure for 3 minutes.
- Allow to release pressure naturally then open the lid.

- Serve and enjoy.

Nutritional Value (Amount per Serving):

- Calories 159
- Fat 7.9 g
- Carbohydrates 4.4 g
- Sugar 0.8 g
- Protein 13.7 g
- Cholesterol 84 mg

FLAVORFUL MAHI MAHI FILLETS

Time: 25 minutes

Serve: 4

Ingredients:

- 6 mahi-mahi fillets
- 2 tbsp lemon juice
- 1 tsp dried oregano
- 28 oz can tomatoes, diced
- 1 onion, sliced
- 3 tbsp butter
- Pepper
- Salt

Directions:

- Add butter into the instant pot and set the pot on sauté mode.
- When instant pot display reads hot then add onion and sauté for 2 minutes.

- Add remaining ingredients except for mahi-mahi fillets and sauté for 3 minutes.
- Now add fish fillets and seal pot with lid. Set instant pot on high pressure for 8 minutes.
- Release pressure using quick release method than open the lid.
- Serve hot and enjoy.

Nutritional Value (Amount per Serving):

- Calories 268
- Fat 8.8 g
- Carbohydrates 13.1 g
- Sugar 8.1 g
- Protein 33.8 g
- Cholesterol 83 mg

FLAVORS COD

Time: 25 minutes

Serve: 2

Ingredients:

- 2 cod steaks
- 1 tbsp balsamic vinegar
- 1/2 tbsp soy sauce
- 2 tbsp lemon pepper seasoning
- 1/4 cup sherry

Directions:

- Mix together in a bowl, sherry, lemon pepper seasoning, soy sauce, and balsamic vinegar.
- Add cod steaks and marinate for 20 minutes.
- Transfer marinated cod steaks in the instant pot. Seal pot with lid and select high pressure for 6 minutes.
- Allow to release pressure naturally then open the lid.
- Serve and enjoy.

Nutritional Value (Amount per Serving):

- Calories 60
- Fat 0.3 g
- Carbohydrates 4.5 g
- Sugar 0.1 g
- Protein 10.5 g
- Cholesterol 40 mg

SIMPLE LEMON GARLIC SHRIMP

Time: 15 minutes

Serve: 3

Ingredients:

- 1 lb large shrimp
- 1 tsp paprika
- 2 lemons, sliced
- 4 garlic cloves, minced
- 3 tbsp butter

Directions:

- Set instant pot on sauté mode and add butter into the pot.
- When instant pot display reads hot then add garlic and sauté for 1 minute.
- Add shrimp, paprika, and lemon slices, and stirs well.
- Seal pot with lid and select high pressure for 4 minutes.
- Allow to release pressure naturally then open the lid.
- Serve and enjoy.

Nutritional Value (Amount per Serving):

- Calories 231
- Fat 11.6 g
- Carbohydrates 4.4 g
- Sugar 0.1 g
- Protein 28.8 g
- Cholesterol 247 mg

PARMESAN TILAPIA

Time: 20 minutes

Serve: 2

Ingredients:

- 2 tilapia fillets
- 2 tbsp lemon juice
- 2 tbsp mayonnaise
- 1/2 cup parmesan cheese, grated
- Pepper
- Salt

Directions:

- In a bowl, mix together mayonnaise, lemon juice, pepper, and salt and marinate tilapia in this mixture.
- Place marinated tilapia fillets into the instant pot.
- Seal pot with lid and select high pressure for 7 minutes.
- Allow to release pressure naturally then open the lid.

- Top with grated parmesan cheese and set the pot on sauté mode for 3 minutes.
- Serve and enjoy.

Nutritional Value (Amount per Serving):

- Calories 345
- Fat 16.6 g
- Carbohydrates 3.9 g
- Sugar 1.3 g
- Protein 48.3 g
- Cholesterol 121 mg

COCONUT SCALLOPS CURRY

Time: 25 minutes

Serve: 4

Ingredients:

- 1 lb scallops
- 1 1/2 cup chicken broth
- 1 tsp curry powder
- 1 tsp vinegar
- 1 cup coconut milk
- 1 tsp soy sauce
- 1/2 tsp nutmeg powder
- 1/2 cup Thai red curry paste
- 1 tbsp olive oil
- 1/2 tsp salt

Directions:

- Set instant pot on sauté mode and add olive oil into the pot.

- When instant pot display reads hot then add scallops and sauté for 3 minutes.
- Add remaining ingredients and stir well.
- Seal pot with lid and select high pressure for 6 minutes.
- Release pressure using quick release method than open the lid.
- Serve and enjoy.

Nutritional Value (Amount per Serving):

- Calories 405
- Fat 28.2 g
- Carbohydrates 12.7 g
- Sugar 2.3 g
- Protein 22.4 g
- Cholesterol 37 mg

SWEET & SOUR FISH

Time: 20 minutes

Serve: 3

Ingredients:

- 1 lb fish chunks
- 1 tbsp vinegar
- 1 tbsp soy sauce
- 1/2 tbsp sugar
- 1 tbsp olive oil
- Pepper
- Salt

Directions:

- Add oil into the instant pot and set the instant pot on sauté mode.
- When instant pot display reads hot then add fish chunks and sauté for 3 minutes.
- Add remaining ingredients and stir well to mix.

- Seal pot with lid and select high pressure for 6 minutes.
- Allow to release pressure naturally then open the lid.
- Stir well and serve.

Nutritional Value (Amount per Serving):

- Calories 402
- Fat 23.3 g
- Carbohydrates 28.1 g
- Sugar 2.1 g
- Protein 22.5 g
- Cholesterol 51 mg

SIMPLE SHRIMP SCAMPI

Time: 15 minutes

Serve: 2

Ingredients:

- 3/4 lb jumbo shrimp, peeled and deveined
- 1 tsp lemon juice
- 2 tbsp parsley, chopped
- 3 tbsp butter
- 2 garlic cloves, chopped
- 2 tbsp dry white wine
- 1/8 tsp black pepper
- 1 tsp kosher salt

Directions:

- Add shrimp, garlic, wine, pepper, and salt into the instant pot and stir well.
- Seal pot with lid and select high pressure for 1 minute.
- Release pressure using quick release method than open the lid.

- Transfer shrimp to a bowl, leaving juices behind.
- Set pot on sauté mode and simmer liquid until reduced half.
- Add butter and stir until melted. Return shrimp to pot and stir well.
- Add lemon juice and parsley and toss to combine.
- Serve and enjoy.

Nutritional Value (Amount per Serving):

- Calories 293
- Fat 17.4 g
- Carbohydrates 1.8 g
- Sugar 3.3 g
- Protein 30.9 g
- Cholesterol 395 mg

CREAMY COCONUT SHRIMP CURRY

Time: 10 minutes

Serve: 2

Ingredients:

- 2 tbsp coconut milk
- 1 lb frozen shrimp
- 1/2 tsp garam masala
- 1/2 cup water
- 2 tbsp fresh cilantro, chopped
- 1/8 tsp cayenne
- 3/4 cup onion masala
- 1/2 tsp salt

Directions:

- Add all ingredients into the instant pot except coconut milk and cilantro.
- Stir well and seal pot with lid and select high pressure for 1 minute.

- Release pressure using quick release method than open the lid.
- Stir in coconut milk and garnish with cilantro.
- Serve and enjoy.

Nutritional Value (Amount per Serving):

- Calories 276
- Fat 7.7 g
- Carbohydrates 3 g
- Sugar 0.5 g
- Protein 46.7 g
- Cholesterol 341 mg

CHILI-LIME SALMON

Time: 15 minutes

Serve: 2

Ingredients:

- 2 salmon fillets
- 1 cup water
- 1/2 tsp cumin
- 1/2 tsp paprika
- 1 tbsp parsley, chopped
- 1 tbsp hot water
- 1 tbsp olive oil
- 1 tbsp honey
- 2 garlic cloves, minced
- 1 lime juice
- 1 jalapeno pepper, diced
- Pepper
- Salt

Directions:

- In a bowl, combine together cumin, paprika, parsley, hot water, olive oil, honey, garlic, lime juice, and jalapeno. Set aside.
- Pour water into the instant pot then place trivet.
- Place salmon fillets on trivet and season with pepper and salt.
- Seal pot with lid and select steam mode and cook on high pressure for 5 minutes.
- Release pressure using quick release method than open the lid.
- Transfer salmon to a serving dish and drizzle with bowl mixture.
- Serve and enjoy.

Nutritional Value (Amount per Serving):

- Calories 338
- Fat 18.3 g
- Carbohydrates 10.7 g
- Sugar 9 g
- Protein 35.1 g
- Cholesterol 78 mg

CHAPTER 7: MEAT RECIPES

TASTY SALSA CHICKEN

Time: 30 minutes

Serve: 4

Ingredients:

- 2 chicken breasts, skinless and boneless
- 4 oz Mexican blend cheese, shredded
- 1 cup long grain rice, rinsed
- 1/2 tsp ground coriander
- 1/2 tsp cumin
- 1 cup chicken stock
- 16 oz salsa
- 1 garlic clove, minced
- 1 small onion, diced
- 1 tbsp olive oil
- 1/4 tsp salt

Directions:

- Add olive oil into the instant pot and set the instant pot on sauté mode.
- Add onion and sauté until translucent, about 4 minutes.
- Add garlic and sauté for 15 seconds. Turn off the instant pot.
- Add salsa, rice, ground coriander, cumin, chicken stock, pepper, and salt. Stir well.
- Seal instant pot with lid. Select pressure cook mode and set it to high and set the timer for 10 minutes.
- Allow to release pressure naturally then open the lid carefully.
- Shred the chicken with a fork and stir well.
- Transfer salsa chicken to the bowl and add shredded cheese and mix well.
- Serve and enjoy.

Nutritional Value (Amount per Serving):

- Calories 485
- Fat 18.1 g
- Carbohydrates 47.6 g
- Sugar 5.8 g
- Protein 32.7 g
- Cholesterol 95 mg

SPICY PORK CARNITAS

Time: 40 minutes

Serve: 4

Ingredients:

- 1 1/2 lbs pork shoulder, cut into chunks
- 1/3 cup orange juice
- 4 garlic cloves, minced
- 1/2 cinnamon stick
- 1 bay leaf
- 1/2 small onion, chopped
- 1/8 tsp cayenne powder
- 1 tsp oregano
- 1 tsp paprika
- 2 tsp chili powder
- 1 tbsp cumin
- 2 tbsp olive oil
- 1/4 tsp pepper
- 1 tsp salt

Directions:

- In a large bowl, add olive oil, cayenne pepper, coriander powder, oregano, paprika, chili powder, cumin, pepper, and salt. Mix well.
- Add meat chunks to the spice mixture and toss well.
- Add meat mixture into the instant pot and set the instant pot on sauté mode.
- Cook meat chunks until browned then remove from pot and set aside.
- Add onion, cinnamon stick, and bay leaf and cook until onion is softened. Stir occasionally.
- Add garlic and sauté for 15 seconds, stirring constantly.
- Add orange juice and stir well. Return meat into the pot and mix well.
- Seal instant pot with lid and select pressure cook mode and set the timer for 30 minutes.
- Allow to release pressure naturally then open the lid.
- Stir well and shred meat using a fork.
- Serve and enjoy.

Nutritional Value (Amount per Serving):

- Calories 587
- Fat 44.1 g
- Carbohydrates 6 g
- Sugar 2.3 g
- Protein 40.6 g
- Cholesterol 153 mg

TENDER & JUICY CHICKEN BREASTS

Time: 20 minutes

Serve: 3

Ingredients:

- 3 chicken breasts, skinless and boneless
- 1 cup water
- 1/8 tsp dried basil
- 1/8 tsp dried oregano
- 1/4 tsp garlic powder
- 1 tbsp olive oil
- 1/8 tsp pepper
- 1/4 tsp salt

Directions:

- Add oil into the instant pot and set the instant pot on sauté mode.
- Season chicken breasts with basil, oregano, garlic, powder, pepper, and salt.

- When instant pot display reads hot then place season chicken breasts into the pot and cook for 3-4 minutes on each side.
- Remove chicken breasts from pot and place on a plate.
- Add 1 cup water into the pot then place trivet.
- Place chicken on a trivet. Seal instant pot with lid and select high pressure for 5 minutes.
- Allow to release pressure naturally for 5 minutes then release using quick release method.
- Open the lid carefully and serve.

Nutritional Value (Amount per Serving):

- Calories 319
- Fat 15.5 g
- Carbohydrates 0.3 g
- Sugar 0.1 g
- Protein 42.3 g
- Cholesterol 130 mg

PORK CHOPS

Time: 35 minutes

Serve: 4

Ingredients:

- 4 pork chops
- 2 tbsp Dijon mustard
- 1 tbsp fresh rosemary, chopped
- 2 tbsp olive oil
- Pepper
- Salt

Directions:

- Rub pork chops with Dijon mustard, rosemary, pepper, and salt.
- Add olive oil and pork chops into the instant pot.
- Seal pot with lid and select high pressure for 15 minutes.
- Allow to release pressure naturally then open the lid.
- Serve and enjoy.

Nutritional Value (Amount per Serving):

- Calories 324
- Fat 27.3 g
- Carbohydrates 1 g
- Sugar 0.1 g
- Protein 18.4 g
- Cholesterol 69 mg

DELICIOUS CHICKEN WITH PINEAPPLE

Time: 20 minutes

Serve: 2

Ingredients:

- 2 chicken drumsticks, trimmed
- 1/2 tbsp lime juice
- 1/2 cup pineapple, chopped
- 1 cup whipping cream
- 1 tsp red pepper flakes
- 1/2 tsp ground mustard
- 1 tbsp brown sugar
- 2 tbsp water
- 2 tbsp coconut milk
- 1 tbsp apple cider vinegar
- 1/2 cup tomato sauce
- Pepper
- Salt

Directions:

- In a large bowl, mix together whipping cream, red pepper flakes, ground mustard, brown sugar, water, coconut milk, vinegar, tomato sauce, pepper, and salt.
- Add chicken drumsticks in whipping cream mixture and coat well.
- Add pineapple into the instant pot then arrange chicken drumsticks over the pineapple pieces.
- Pour remaining whipping cream mixture over the drumsticks evenly.
- Seal pot with lid and select high pressure for 10 minutes.
- Release pressure using quick release method than open the lid.
- Drizzle chicken drumsticks with lime juice and serve.

Nutritional Value (Amount per Serving):

- Calories 348
- Fat 25.3 g
- Carbohydrates 16.6 g
- Sugar 11.8 g
- Protein 15.7 g
- Cholesterol 107 mg

HEALTHY SWISS BEEF

Time: 1 hour 10 minutes

Serve: 3

Ingredients:

- 1 lb beef
- 1 tbsp dried oregano
- 1 cup coriander leaves
- 1 tbsp celery
- 2 tbsp allspice
- 1 tbsp ginger, minced
- 3 garlic cloves, minced
- 2 onions, chopped
- 1 bell pepper, chopped
- 2 tbsp olive oil
- 1 tbsp pepper
- 1 tbsp salt

Directions:

- Add olive oil into the instant pot and set pot on sauté mode.
- When the display reads hot then add garlic and sauté for 2 minutes.
- Add beef and remaining ingredients and mix well.
- Seal pot with lid and select high pressure for 40 minutes.
- Allow to release pressure naturally then open the lid carefully.
- Serve and enjoy.

Nutritional Value (Amount per Serving):

- Calories 436
- Fat 19.7 g
- Carbohydrates 17.6 g
- Sugar 5.4 g
- Protein 48.2 g
- Cholesterol 135 mg

DELICIOUS BACON CHILI

Time: 40 minutes

Serve: 2

Ingredients:

- 2 bacon slices, chopped
- 1/4 cup sour cream
- 1 oz tomato sauce
- 7 oz can roasted tomatoes
- 1 tsp ground cumin
- 1/2 tbsp smoked paprika
- 2 garlic cloves, minced
- 1/2 onion, chopped
- 1/2 tbsp chili powder
- 1/2 bell pepper, chopped

Directions:

- Add bacon into the instant pot and set the pot on sauté mode.

- Sauté bacon for 3 minutes. Remove bacon from pot and place on a paper towel.
- Add onion, garlic, and bell pepper to the pot and sauté for 2 minutes.
- Add spices and cook for 5 minutes.
- Stir in cooked bacon, tomato sauce, and roasted can tomatoes.
- Seal pot with lid and select bean/chili mode and set the timer for 20 minutes.
- Allow to release pressure naturally then open the lid.
- Top with sour cream and serve.

Nutritional Value (Amount per Serving):

- Calories 232
- Fat 14.9 g
- Carbohydrates 15.4 g
- Sugar 6.1 g
- Protein 10.4 g
- Cholesterol 34 mg

EASY ORANGE CHICKEN

Time: 20 minutes

Serve: 4

Ingredients:

- 1 lb chicken breast, cut into cubes
- 3 tbsp cornstarch
- 3 tbsp water
- 1/4 cup soy sauce
- 1/3 cup brown sugar
- 1 cup orange juice
- 8 oz tomato sauce
- 1 tsp garlic, minced
- 2 tbsp olive oil
- Pepper
- Salt

Directions:

- In a small bowl, mix together 3 tbsp water and cornstarch and set aside.
- Set instant pot on sauté mode and add oil into the pot.
- When instant pot display reads hot then add garlic and chicken. Season chicken with pepper and salt and sauté chicken until brown.
- Add soy sauce, brown sugar, orange juice, and tomato sauce and stir well.
- Seal pot with lid and select high pressure for 7 minutes.
- Release pressure using quick release method than open the lid.
- Add cornstarch mixture into the pot and stir until thickens.
- Serve and enjoy.

Nutritional Value (Amount per Serving):

- Calories 309
- Fat 10.1 g
- Carbohydrates 28.3 g
- Sugar 19.6 g
- Protein 26.3 g
- Cholesterol 73 mg

TASTY BUTTER CHICKEN

Time: 20 minutes

Serve: 3

Ingredients:

- 1 lb chicken breast, cubed
- 3 tbsp cornstarch
- 1 green pepper, chopped
- 14 oz tomato sauce
- 1/4 tsp cumin
- 1/4 tsp cayenne pepper
- 1 tsp paprika
- 1 tsp curry powder
- 1 tsp ginger, minced
- 4 tsp garlic, minced
- 1 small onion, diced
- 2 tbsp butter
- 1/4 tsp pepper
- 1 tsp salt

Directions:

- In a small bowl, mix together 1/4 cup water and cornstarch and set aside.
- Add butter into the instant pot and set the pot on sauté mode.
- Once butter is melted then add garlic, onion, and chicken and sauté for 3-5 minutes or until chicken cooked from outside.
- Add spices, green pepper, and tomato sauce to the pot and mix well.
- Seal pot with lid and select high pressure for 7 minutes.
- Release pressure using quick release method than open the lid.
- Add cornstarch mixture and stir well.
- Serve and enjoy.

Nutritional Value (Amount per Serving):

- Calories 333
- Fat 12.1 g
- Carbohydrates 21.2 g
- Sugar 7.7 g
- Protein 35 g
- Cholesterol 117 mg

YUMMY MANGO CHICKEN

Time: 25 minutes

Serve: 2

Ingredients:

- 2 chicken breasts, skinless and boneless
- 1 garlic clove, minced
- 1/2 tsp ginger, grated
- 1 lime juice
- 1 ripe mango, peeled and diced
- 1 tbsp turmeric
- 1/2 cup chicken broth
- 1/2 tsp pepper
- 1/2 tsp salt

Directions:

- Add chicken into the instant pot and top with mango.
- Add lime juice and chicken broth over the chicken breast and mango.

- Top with turmeric, pepper, and salt.
- Seal pot with lid and select high pressure for 15 minutes.
- Allow to release pressure naturally then open the lid.
- Shred the chicken using a fork and stir well.
- Serve with rice and enjoy.

Nutritional Value (Amount per Serving):

- Calories 405
- Fat 12.2 g
- Carbohydrates 28.8 g
- Sugar 23.3 g
- Protein 45.3 g
- Cholesterol 130 mg

SHREDDED MEXICAN CHICKEN

Time: 30 minutes

Serve: 4

Ingredients:

- 1 lb chicken thighs, skinless and boneless
- 1/2 tsp cayenne pepper
- 1 tsp cumin
- 1 tsp oregano
- 1 tbsp garlic, minced
- 2 tbsp butter
- 1 lime juice
- 4 chipotle peppers in adobo sauce
- 1 cup chicken broth
- 1 cup water
- 1 tsp pepper
- 1 tsp salt

Directions:

- Add butter into the instant pot and set the pot on sauté mode.
- Once butter is melted then add garlic and sauté for 1 minute.
- Add chicken and cook for 4 minutes. Add broth, lime juice, spices, and peppers. Stir well.
- Seal pot with lid and select high pressure for 15 minutes.
- Release pressure using quick release method than open the lid.
- Shred the chicken using a fork and serve.

Nutritional Value (Amount per Serving):

- Calories 284
- Fat 14.7 g
- Carbohydrates 1.9 g
- Sugar 0.2 g
- Protein 34.4 g
- Cholesterol 116 mg

CASHEW BUTTER CHICKEN

Time: 20 minutes

Serve: 3

Ingredients:

- 1 lb chicken breast, cut into chunks
- 1 garlic clove, minced
- 1/4 cup chicken broth
- 1/2 tbsp sriracha
- 2 tbsp rice vinegar
- 2 tbsp honey
- 2 tbsp coconut aminos
- 1/4 cup smooth cashew butter

Directions:

- Add chicken chunks into the instant pot.
- In a small bowl, mix together cashew butter, garlic, broth, sriracha, vinegar, honey, and coconut aminos.
- Pour cashew butter mixture on top of chicken.

- Seal pot with lid and select high pressure for 7 minutes.
- Release pressure using quick release method than open the lid.
- Stir well and serve.

Nutritional Value (Amount per Serving):

- Calories 294
- Fat 9.2 g
- Carbohydrates 16.2 g
- Sugar 12.1 g
- Protein 34.3 g
- Cholesterol 97 mg

QUICK FLAVORFUL CHILI

Time: 35 minutes

Serve: 3

Ingredients:

- 1 lb ground beef
- 1 1/2 tbsp water
- 1 tbsp cornstarch
- 7 oz can creamed corn
- 18 oz can kidney beans, rinsed and drained
- 1 bay leaf
- 1/2 cup chicken stock
- 14 oz can tomatoes, diced
- 1/2 green pepper, diced
- 1/2 tsp sugar
- 1/8 tsp cayenne
- 1/2 tsp oregano
- 1/2 tsp cumin
- 1 tbsp chili powder
- 1/2 tbsp garlic, minced

- 1/2 onion, diced
- 1/2 tsp black pepper
- 1 1/2 tsp salt

Directions:

- In a small bowl, stir together cornstarch and water and set aside.
- Set instant pot on sauté mode. Add meat, pepper, onion, and salt into the instant pot and cook until browned.
- Add garlic and sauté for 30 seconds. Add remaining ingredients except for beans and cornstarch mixture and stir well.
- Seal pot with lid and select high pressure for 12 minutes.
- Allow to release pressure naturally then open the lid.
- Set pot on sauté mode. Add cornstarch mixture and beans and stir until thickens, about 3 minutes.
- Serve and enjoy.

Nutritional Value (Amount per Serving):

- Calories 542
- Fat 11.1 g
- Carbohydrates 53.1 g
- Sugar 9.9 g
- Protein 58.8 g
- Cholesterol 135 mg

CREAMY & SAVORY CHICKEN SCAMPI

Time: 15 minutes

Serve: 4

Ingredients:

- 1 lb chicken breast, cubed
- 3 cups water
- 16 oz pasta
- 1 tbsp olive oil
- 1 cup white wine
- 1 cup heavy cream
- 4 garlic cloves, chopped
- 1 tbsp Italian seasoning
- 1 onion, chopped
- 3 bell peppers, sliced

Directions:

- Add oil into the instant pot and set the pot on sauté mode.

- When instant pot display reads hot then add garlic and onion and sauté for a minute.
- Add chicken and cook for 2-3 minutes. Add seasoning and white wine. Stir well.
- Add pasta and enough water to cover the pasta.
- Seal pot with lid and select high pressure for 4 minutes.
- Release pressure using quick release method than open the lid.
- Set pot on sauté mode and stir in heavy cream and cook for 1-2 minutes.
- Serve and enjoy.

Nutritional Value (Amount per Serving):

- Calories 693
- Fat 21.4 g
- Carbohydrates 75.2 g
- Sugar 6.5 g
- Protein 38.9 g
- Cholesterol 199 mg

SPICY GROUND MEAT

Time: 20 minutes

Serve: 4

Ingredients:

- 1 lb ground beef
- 1/2 tsp turmeric
- 1 tsp garam masala
- 4 green cardamoms
- 3 cinnamon sticks pieces
- 1 tbsp garlic
- 1 tbsp ginger, minced
- 1 cup onion, chopped
- 1 cup frozen peas
- 1/4 cup water
- 1/2 tsp cumin
- 1/2 tsp ground coriander
- 1/2 tsp cayenne pepper
- 1 tbsp butter
- 1 tsp salt

Directions:

- Add butter into the instant pot and set pot on sauté mode.
- Once butter is melted then add cardamom and cinnamon sticks and sauté for 10 seconds.
- Add ginger, garlic, and onion and cook for 5 minutes.
- Add ground beef and sauté for 3-4 minutes. Add spices and water and stir well.
- Seal pot with lid and select high pressure for 5 minutes.
- Allow to release pressure naturally then open the lid.
- Add peas and stir well.
- Serve and enjoy.

Nutritional Value (Amount per Serving):

- Calories 289
- Fat 10.3 g
- Carbohydrates 10.5 g
- Sugar 3.2 g
- Protein 37.2 g
- Cholesterol 109 mg

CLASSIC CHICKEN ADOBO

Time: 30 minutes

Serve: 2

Ingredients:

- 1/2 lb chicken thighs bone-in and skin-on
- 1 bay leaf, crushed
- 1/2 tsp red pepper flakes
- 1/2 tsp black peppercorns, crushed
- 1/2 tbsp brown sugar
- 1 tbsp garlic, minced
- 1 tbsp olive oil
- 1 tbsp soy sauce
- 1/4 cup white vinegar

Directions:

- In a bowl, combine together vinegar, bay leaf, red pepper flakes, black peppercorns, sugar, garlic, soy sauce, and oil.

- Place chicken in a bowl and coat well with the sauce and set aside for 30 minutes.
- Add marinated chicken with marinade into the instant pot.
- Seal pot with lid and select high pressure for 8 minutes.
- Release pressure using quick release method than open the lid.
- Remove chicken from pot and place on a baking tray and broil for 2-3 minutes.
- Meanwhile set the instant pot on sauté mode and cook until sauce thickened, about 2-3 minutes.
- Pour sauce over chicken and serve.

Nutritional Value (Amount per Serving):

- Calories 304
- Fat 15.5 g
- Carbohydrates 5.1 g
- Sugar 2.5 g
- Protein 33.7 g
- Cholesterol 101 mg

CHAPTER 8: VEGETARIAN RECIPES

LOW-CARB BRUSSELS SPROUTS

Time: 20 minutes

Serve: 3

Ingredients:

- 1 lb Brussels sprouts, trimmed and halved
- 1/4 cup apple cider vinegar
- 1/4 cup soy sauce
- 4 bacon slices, chopped
- 1/2 tsp pepper
- 1/2 tsp sea salt

Directions:

- Set instant pot on sauté mode. When the display reads hot then add bacon and cook for 5 minutes. Stir frequently.
- Add Brussels sprouts, vinegar, soy sauce, pepper, and salt. Stir well to mix.
- Seal pot with lid and select high pressure for 4 minutes.
- Release pressure using quick release method than open the lid.

- Stir well and serve.

Nutritional Value (Amount per Serving):

- Calories 219
- Fat 11.1 g
- Carbohydrates 16.2 g
- Sugar 3.7 g
- Protein 15.9 g
- Cholesterol 28 mg

ARTICHOKE WITH SPICY DIP

Time: 30 minutes

Serve: 2

Ingredients:

- 2 large artichokes, Cut the stem and rinsed
- 1 tbsp olive oil
- 1 1/2 cups water
- Pepper
- Salt
- For dip:
- 1/4 tsp cayenne
- 2 garlic cloves, minced
- 1 tbsp Dijon mustard
- 5 tbsp mayonnaise

Directions:

- Pour water into the instant pot then place trivet into the pot.

- Place artichoke on a trivet. Seal pot with lid and select high pressure for 10 minutes.
- Allow to release pressure naturally then open the lid.
- Meanwhile, in a small bowl, combine together all dip ingredients until smooth.
- Once artichokes are cool then slice each artichoke in half and brush with olive oil. Season with pepper and salt.
- Serve with dip and enjoy.

Nutritional Value (Amount per Serving):

- Calories 290
- Fat 19.9 g
- Carbohydrates 27.4 g
- Sugar 4.1 g
- Protein 6.2 g
- Cholesterol 10 mg

PERFECT WHITE BEAN SALAD

Time: 30 minutes

Serve: 3

Ingredients:

- 15 oz can cannellini beans, rinsed
- 1/4 small onion, sliced
- 1/2 bell pepper, chopped
- 1 tsp Dijon mustard
- 1 tbsp olive oil
- 1 tsp fresh thyme
- 1 tbsp vinegar
- Pepper
- Salt

Directions:

- Add bean into the instant pot and season with pepper and salt.
- Seal pot with lid and select high pressure for 20 minutes.

- Allow to release pressure naturally then open the lid.
- Add remaining ingredients and mix well.
- Serve and enjoy.

Nutritional Value (Amount per Serving):

- Calories 183
- Fat 4.8 g
- Carbohydrates 25.3 g
- Sugar 2.4 g
- Protein 9.1 g
- Cholesterol 0 mg

HEARTY BAKED BEANS

Time: 35 minutes

Serve: 4

Ingredients:

- 7.5 oz can northern beans, rinsed and drained
- 7.5 oz can pinto beans, rinsed and drained
- 7.5 oz can kidney beans, rinsed and drained
- 1/2 tsp chili powder
- 1/2 tbsp yellow mustard
- 1/4 cup dark brown sugar
- 6 tbsp water
- 1/4 cup ketchup
- 1/2 onion, diced

Directions:

- Add all ingredients into the instant pot and stir well to combine.
- Seal pot with lid and select high pressure for 8 minutes.

- Allow to release pressure naturally then open the lid.
- Stir well and serve.

Nutritional Value (Amount per Serving):

- Calories 195
- Fat 1.3 g
- Carbohydrates 39.4 g
- Sugar 14.4 g
- Protein 8.1 g
- Cholesterol 0 mg

KALE LENTIL CURRY

Time: 30 minutes

Serve: 2

Ingredients:

- 1/2 cup red lentils, rinsed and drained
- 1 cup baby kale
- 1/4 cup coconut milk
- 1 1/4 cup water
- 1/2 tbsp ground ginger
- 1/2 tbsp curry powder
- 1/2 bell pepper, chopped
- 1 carrot, chopped
- 1/2 onion, chopped
- 1 tsp olive oil
- 1/2 tsp sea salt

Directions:

- Add oil into the instant pot and set the pot on sauté mode.

- Add onion, bell pepper, and carrots and sauté for 10 minutes.
- Add lentils, ginger, curry powder, and salt and sauté for 1 minute.
- Add water and stir well. Seal pot with lid and select high pressure for 10 minutes.
- Allow to release pressure naturally then open the lid.
- Add kale and coconut milk and stir until kale is wilted. Season with pepper and salt.
- Serve over rice and enjoy.

Nutritional Value (Amount per Serving):

- Calories 313
- Fat 10.5 g
- Carbohydrates 42.5 g
- Sugar 6.2 g
- Protein 15 g
- Cholesterol 0 mg

HEALTHY SPINACH LENTIL

Time: 50 minutes

Serve: 3

Ingredients:

- 4 oz baby spinach
- 1 tbsp lemon juice
- 1/2 lb green lentils
- 1/2 tbsp curry powder
- 2 1/2 cups vegetable broth
- 7 oz can roasted tomatoes
- 7 oz can coconut milk
- 2 tbsp curry paste
- 1/2 tbsp garlic, minced
- 2 tbsp onion, diced
- 1/2 tbsp ginger, grated
- 1/2 Serrano pepper, diced
- 1 tbsp olive oil
- 1/4 tsp pepper
- 1/2 tsp sea salt

Directions:

- Add oil into the instant pot and set pot on sauté mode.
- Add ginger, onion, and Serrano pepper and sauté for 3-4 minutes.
- Add garlic, curry powder, and curry paste and sauté for 2 minutes.
- Add remaining ingredients except for spinach and stir to combine.
- Seal pot with lid and select high pressure for 15 minutes.
- Allow to release pressure naturally then open the lid.
- Add spinach and stir until spinach is wilted.
- Serve and enjoy.

Nutritional Value (Amount per Serving):

- Calories 488
- Fat 16.7 g
- Carbohydrates 57.3 g
- Sugar 5.5 g
- Protein 27.2 g
- Cholesterol 0 mg

VEGAN BLACK EYED PEAS

Time: 25 minutes

Serve: 3

Ingredients:

- 1/2 cup dry black-eyed peas
- 1 tbsp peanut butter
- 1 cup Swiss chard
- 1 1/4 cup vegetable stock
- 1/2 cup can tomatoes
- 1/2 cup onion, chopped
- 1/2 tsp pepper
- 1/2 tsp salt

Directions:

- Add all ingredients except peanut butter into the instant pot and stir well.
- Add peanut butter on top. Seal pot with lid and select high pressure for 15 minutes.

- Allow to release pressure naturally then open the lid.
- Stir well and serve.

Nutritional Value (Amount per Serving):

- Calories 115
- Fat 3.6 g
- Carbohydrates 21.7 g
- Sugar 4.3 g
- Protein 8.2 g
- Cholesterol 0 mg

CREAMY GREEN PEAS

Time: 25 minutes

Serve: 3

Ingredients:

- 1 cup green peas, frozen and thawed
- 1 cup heavy cream
- 2 tbsp butter
- 1 cup vegetable stock
- Pepper
- Salt

Directions:

- Add butter into the instant pot and set the pot on sauté mode.
- Once butter is melted then add peas and sauté for 2 minutes.
- Add stock, heavy cream, and salt. Stir well.
- Seal pot with lid and select high pressure for 6 minutes.
- Allow to release pressure naturally then open the lid.

- Puree the pea mixture using an immersion blender until smooth and creamy.
- Serve and enjoy.

Nutritional Value (Amount per Serving):

- Calories 245
- Fat 23.3 g
- Carbohydrates 8.8 g
- Sugar 3.5 g
- Protein 3.5 g
- Cholesterol 75 mg

SOUTHWEST BLACK BEANS

Time: 45 minutes

Serve: 4

Ingredients:

- 1 cup dry black beans, rinsed
- 3 cups vegetable broth
- 1/2 tsp coriander powder
- 1 tsp chili powder
- 1 tsp oregano
- 1/2 tsp smoked paprika
- 2 tsp cumin
- 1 bay leaf
- 3 garlic cloves, minced
- 1/2 small onion, diced
- 3 bacon slices, chopped
- 1/4 tsp pepper
- 1/4 tsp kosher salt

Directions:

- Set instant pot on sauté mode.
- Once display reads hot then add bacon and cook until done.
- Add onion and sauté for few minutes. Add garlic, coriander powder, chili powder, oregano, paprika, cumin, bay leaf, pepper, and salt. Stir well.
- Add broth and beans and stir well.
- Seal instant pot with lid and select pressure cook mode and set the timer for 35 minutes.
- Once the timer goes off then allow to release pressure naturally then open the lid.
- Stir well and serve.

Nutritional Value (Amount per Serving):

- Calories 286
- Fat 8.1 g
- Carbohydrates 34 g
- Sugar 2.1 g
- Protein 20 g
- Cholesterol 16 mg

CHAPTER 9: SOUP & STEW

DELICIOUS BEEF STEW

Time: 40 minutes

Serve: 4

Ingredients:

- 1 1/2 lbs beef stew meat, cut into cubes
- 1 cup water
- 1/2 tsp cayenne pepper
- 2 tsp smoked paprika
- 1/4 tsp ground nutmeg
- 1 tsp ground cumin
- 1 tbsp coriander powder
- 1 tbsp garam masala
- 1/4 tsp turmeric powder
- 1/2 tsp sugar
- 3 tbsp tomato paste
- 1/2 tsp ginger powder
- 1/2 tsp garlic powder
- 1 onion, chopped
- 3 tbsp butter

- 1 tsp salt

Directions:

- Add butter into the instant pot and set pot on sauté mode.
- Once butter is melted then add onion, turmeric, ginger powder, garlic powder, and salt and sauté until onion is lightly browned.
- Add all dry spices, 1/4 cup water, and tomato paste and stir for a minute.
- Add meat and remaining water. Stir well and seal pot with lid and select stew/meat setting for 30 minutes.
- Allow to release pressure naturally then open the lid.
- Add sugar and stir well.
- Serve and enjoy.

Nutritional Value (Amount per Serving):

- Calories 424
- Fat 19.7 g
- Carbohydrates 6.9 g
- Sugar 3.4 g
- Protein 52.9 g
- Cholesterol 175 mg

EASY SALMON STEW

Time: 15 minutes

Serve: 3

Ingredients:

- 1 lb salmon fillet, cubed
- 1 onion, chopped
- 1 cup fish broth
- 1 tbsp butter
- Pepper
- Salt

Directions:

- Add all ingredients into the instant pot and stir well to mix.
- Seal pot with lid and select high pressure for 6 minutes.
- Allow to release pressure naturally then open the lid.
- Stir well and serve.

Nutritional Value (Amount per Serving):

- Calories 261
- Fat 13.7 g
- Carbohydrates 3.7 g
- Sugar 1.8 g
- Protein 31.4 g
- Cholesterol 77 mg

LENTIL CHICKEN SOUP

Time: 45 minutes

Serve: 4

Ingredients:

- 6 oz chicken thighs, skinless and boneless
- 1/2 lb dried lentils
- 1/4 tsp paprika
- 1/8 tsp oregano
- 1/2 tsp cumin
- 1/2 tsp garlic powder
- 1 small tomato, diced
- 2 tbsp cilantro, chopped
- 1 scallion, chopped
- 1/2 small onion, chopped
- 3 1/2 cups water
- 1/4 tsp salt

Directions:

- Add all ingredients into the instant pot and stir well.
- Seal pot with lid and select soup mode and set the timer for 30 minutes.
- Allow to release pressure naturally then open the lid.
- Shred the chicken using a fork and stir well.
- Serve and enjoy.

Nutritional Value (Amount per Serving):

- Calories 293
- Fat 3.9 g
- Carbohydrates 36.5 g
- Protein 27.5 g
- Cholesterol 38 mg

BEST CHICKEN NOODLE SOUP

Time: 15 minutes

Serve: 3

Ingredients:

- 1/2 lb chicken breast, cubed
- 1/2 half and half
- 1/2 cup cheddar cheese, shredded
- 4 oz spaghetti, uncooked and break in half
- 2 cups chicken broth
- 1/2 packet ranch seasoning
- 1/2 cup celery, chopped
- 1/2 cup carrots, chopped
- 1/2 small onion, diced
- 3 bacon slices, chopped
- Pepper
- Salt

Directions:

- Set instant pot on sauté mode.
- When pot display reads hot then add chicken, onion, and bacon. Stir frequently.
- Add ranch seasoning, celery, carrots, and broth and mix well.
- Add spaghetti and press into the broth so the spaghetti is coated with liquid.
- Seal pot with lid and select high pressure for 5 minutes.
- Release pressure using quick release method than open the lid.
- Add cheddar cheese and stir until cheese is melted.
- Add half and half and stir well to combine.
- Serve and enjoy.

Nutritional Value (Amount per Serving):

- Calories 467
- Fat 22.5 g
- Carbohydrates 27 g
- Sugar 2.2 g
- Protein 36.9 g
- Cholesterol 132 mg

DELICIOUS GOULASH

Time: 20 minutes

Serve: 3

Ingredients:

- 1/2 lb beef stew meat, cut into cubes
- 3 oz egg noodles
- 3 cups chicken broth
- 7 oz can tomatoes, diced
- 1 1/2 tbsp paprika
- 1 tsp garlic, minced
- 1/2 onion, chopped
- 1 tbsp olive oil
- 1/8 tsp pepper
- 1/2 tsp salt

Directions:

- Add oil into the instant pot and set the instant pot on sauté mode.

- When instant pot display reads hot then add garlic, onion, and meat and sauté until meat is browned.
- Add paprika, broth, pasta, tomatoes, pepper, and salt. Stir well.
- Seal pot with lid and select high pressure for 5 minutes.
- Release pressure using quick release method than open the lid.
- Stir well and serve.

Nutritional Value (Amount per Serving):

- Calories 291
- Fat 11.8 g
- Carbohydrates 15.4 g
- Protein 30.5 g
- Cholesterol 76 mg

SWEET POTATO STEW

Time: 20 minutes

Serve: 3

Ingredients:

- 1 small sweet potato, peeled and diced
- 1 lime juice
- 7 oz can coconut milk
- 1 tbsp red curry paste
- 1/2 tsp turmeric
- 1 tsp curry powder
- 7 oz can tomatoes, diced
- 1/2 bell pepper, diced
- 1/2 zucchini, diced
- 1 garlic clove, minced
- 1/2 tbsp ginger, minced
- 1 small onion, diced
- 1 tbsp olive oil
- 1/2 tsp sea salt

Directions:

- Add oil into the instant pot and set pot on sauté mode.
- When instant pot display reads hot then add onion and sauté until translucent.
- Add garlic and ginger and sauté for a minute.
- Add remaining ingredients and mix well. Seal pot with lid and select high pressure for 5 minutes.
- Release pressure using quick release method than open the lid.
- Stir well and serve.

Nutritional Value (Amount per Serving):

- Calories 251
- Fat 20.6 g
- Carbohydrates 16.7 g
- Sugar 6.2 g
- Protein 3.5 g
- Cholesterol 0 mg

TASTY POTATO SOUP

Time: 45 minutes

Serve: 3

Ingredients:

- 1 1/2 lbs potatoes, chopped
- 2 cups vegetable stock
- 1 tbsp vinegar
- 1 tbsp garlic, minced
- 1 bay leaf
- 1 medium carrot, peeled and diced
- 1 celery stalk, diced
- 1/2 onion, diced
- 1 tbsp olive oil
- 1/2 tsp black pepper
- 1/2 tbsp sea salt

Directions:

- Add oil into the instant pot and set pot on sauté mode.

- When instant pot display reads hot then add onions, celery, and carrot and cook for 5 minutes.
- Add bay leaf, garlic, and vinegar and cook for 2 minutes.
- Add stock, potatoes, pepper, and salt. Mix well.
- Seal pot with lid and select high pressure for 7 minutes.
- Release pressure using quick release method than open the lid.
- Discard bay leaf and mash well with a masher.
- Stir well and serve.

Nutritional Value (Amount per Serving):

- Calories 226
- Fat 6.3 g
- Carbohydrates 42.1 g
- Sugar 5.9 g
- Protein 4.4 g
- Cholesterol 0 mg

DELICIOUS CORN CHOWDER

Time: 35 minutes

Serve: 4

Ingredients:

- 3/4 cup half and half
- 1/2 tbsp dried parsley
- 1 tbsp sugar
- 1 1/2 cups chicken stock
- 1/2 lb potatoes, chopped
- 2 cups corn
- 2 garlic cloves, minced
- 1/2 onion, chopped
- 3 bacon slices, chopped
- 1/2 tsp pepper
- 1/2 tsp salt

Directions:

- Set instant pot on sauté mode.

- Add bacon to the pot and sauté for 5 minutes. Remove bacon from pot and set aside.
- Add onion and cook until softened. Add garlic and sauté for a minute.
- Add corn and potatoes stir for a minute. Add stock, parsley, sugar, pepper, salt, and half cooked bacon. Stir well.
- Seal pot with lid and select high pressure for 12 minutes.
- Allow to release pressure naturally then open the lid.
- Add half and half and stir. Using blender blend until thickened.
- Garnish with remaining bacon and serve.

Nutritional Value (Amount per Serving):

- Calories 265
- Fat 12.4 g
- Carbohydrates 30.8 g
- Sugar 7.1 g
- Protein 10.6 g
- Cholesterol 32 mg

CREAMY WILD RICE MUSHROOM SOUP

Time: 55 minutes

Serve: 3

Ingredients:

- 4 oz mushrooms, sliced
- 1/2 cup wild rice, uncooked
- 1/4 tsp dried thyme
- 1/2 tsp poultry seasoning
- 2 cups chicken broth
- 1 garlic clove, minced
- 1/2 small onion, chopped
- 2 celery stalks, chopped
- 3 carrots, chopped
- 1/2 tsp salt

Directions:

- Add all ingredients into the instant pot and stir well.
- Seal pot with lid and select high pressure for 40 minutes.

- Release pressure using quick release method than open the lid.
- Stir well and serve.

Nutritional Value (Amount per Serving):

- Calories 162
- Fat 1.4 g
- Carbohydrates 29.6 g
- Sugar 5.4 g
- Protein 9.1 g
- Cholesterol 0 mg

YUMMY TOMATO SOUP

Time: 15 minutes

Serve: 3

Ingredients:

- 15 oz can tomatoes, diced
- 4 tbsp cashew, cut into pieces
- 1 1/2 cups vegetable stock
- 1/2 tbsp basil, dried
- 1 1/2 tbsp quick oats
- 2 garlic cloves, minced
- 15 oz can tomato puree
- Pepper
- Salt

Directions:

- Add all ingredients except pepper and salt into the instant pot and stir well.
- Seal pot with lid and select high pressure for 4 minutes.

- Allow to release pressure naturally then open the lid.
- Puree the soup using a blender until smooth. Season with pepper and salt.
- Serve and enjoy.

Nutritional Value (Amount per Serving):

- Calories 166
- Fat 6.5 g
- Carbohydrates 26.8 g
- Sugar 13 g
- Protein 5.9 g
- Cholesterol 0 mg

TOMATO CABBAGE SOUP

Time: 25 minutes

Serve: 4

Ingredients:

- 1 small cabbage head, chopped
- 3 cups chicken broth
- 28 oz can tomatoes, chopped
- 3 celery stalks, chopped
- 3 carrots, chopped
- 1 tbsp fresh lemon juice
- 3 tbsp apple cider vinegar
- 4 garlic cloves, minced
- 1 onion, chopped

Directions:

- Add all ingredients into the instant pot and stir well.
- Seal pot with lid and select high pressure for 15 minutes.
- Release pressure using quick release method than open the lid.

- Stir and serve.

Nutritional Value (Amount per Serving):

- Calories 155
- Fat 1.3 g
- Carbohydrates 29.8 g
- Sugar 16.7 g
- Protein 8.7 g
- Cholesterol 0 mg

CREAMY COCONUT SQUASH SOUP

Time: 40 minutes

Serve: 2

Ingredients:

- 1 1/2 lbs butternut squash, peeled and cubed
- 1/2 tbsp curry powder
- 1 garlic cloves, minced
- 1/4 cup coconut milk
- 1 1/2 cups water
- 1/2 onion, minced
- 1 tsp olive oil

Directions:

- Add olive oil in the instant pot and set the pot on sauté mode.
- Add onion and sauté until tender. Add curry powder and garlic and sauté for a minute.
- Add butternut squash, water, and salt and stir well.

- Seal pot with lid and select soup setting and set timer for 25 minutes.
- Release pressure using quick release method than open the lid.
- Using blender puree the soup until smooth and creamy.
- Add coconut milk and stir well.
- Serve and enjoy.

Nutritional Value (Amount per Serving):

- Calories 260
- Fat 10.1 g
- Carbohydrates 45.4 g
- Sugar 9.7 g
- Protein 4.7 g
- Cholesterol 0 mg

COCONUT CAULIFLOWER SOUP

Time: 25 minutes

Serve: 4

Ingredients:

- 2 cups cauliflower florets
- 1/8 tsp thyme
- 1 1/3 tbsp curry powder
- 2/3 cups carrots, diced
- 1 cup onion, diced
- 1 1/3 tbsp olive oil
- 2/3 cup cashews, chopped
- 9 oz can coconut milk
- 2 2/3 cups chicken broth
- 1/8 tsp black pepper
- 1/8 tsp salt

Directions:

- Add oil into the instant pot and set the pot on sauté mode.

- Add carrots, onion, and cauliflower into the instant pot and sauté for 5 minutes.
- Add remaining ingredients except for coconut milk and cashews and stir well.
- Seal pot with lid and select high pressure for 10 minutes.
- Allow to release pressure naturally then open the lid.
- Add coconut milk and stir well. Puree the soup using a blender until smooth.
- Top with cashews and serve.

Nutritional Value (Amount per Serving):

- Calories 361
- Fat 30.1 g
- Carbohydrates 18.3 g
- Sugar 5 g
- Protein 9.8 g
- Cholesterol 0 mg

SPICY MUSHROOM SOUP

Time: 15 minutes

Serve: 3

Ingredients:

- 4 cups mushrooms, sliced
- 1/2 cup heavy whipping cream
- 1 tsp dried thyme
- 1 tbsp garlic, minced
- 1 cup chicken broth
- 1 jalapeno pepper, chopped
- 2 onions, sliced
- 1 tsp pepper
- 1 tsp salt

Directions:

- Add all ingredients except whipping cream into the instant pot.
- Seal pot with lid and select high pressure for 10 minutes.

- Allow to release pressure naturally then open the lid.
- Puree the soup using a blender until smooth leaving some mushroom pieces whole.
- Add heavy whipping cream and stir well.
- Serve and enjoy.

Nutritional Value (Amount per Serving):

- Calories 139
- Fat 8.3 g
- Carbohydrates 12.7 g
- Sugar 5.2 g
- Protein 6.1 g
- Cholesterol 27 mg

HEALTHY CARROT SOUP

Time: 15 minutes

Serve: 3

Ingredients:

- 1 lb carrots cut into quarters
- 3 cups chicken stock
- 1 tsp paprika
- 1 tsp ground cumin
- 2 tsp garlic, minced
- 2 tbsp Dijon mustard
- 1/4 cup butter
- Pepper
- Salt

Directions:

- Add 1 cup water into the instant pot and place trivet into the pot.
- Arrange carrots on top of carrots.

- Seal pot with lid and select high pressure for 1 minute.
- Release pressure using quick release method than open the lid.
- Transfer carrots on a dish. Clean instant pot and dry with paper towel.
- Add butter into the instant pot and set the pot on sauté mode.
- Once butter is melted then add remaining ingredients and stir in cooked carrots.
- Seal pot with lid and select high pressure for 4 minutes.
- Allow to release pressure naturally then open the lid.
- Puree the soup using a blender until smooth and creamy.
- Serve hot and enjoy.

Nutritional Value (Amount per Serving):

- Calories 222
- Fat 16.6 g
- Carbohydrates 17.5 g
- Sugar 8.4 g
- Protein 2.9 g
- Cholesterol 41 mg

CHEESE BROCCOLI SOUP

Time: 30 minutes

Serve: 3

Ingredients:

- 2 1/2 cups broccoli florets
- 1/4 cup parmesan cheese, shredded
- 1/2 cup pepper jack cheese, shredded
- 1/2 cup Colby jack cheese, shredded
- 2 American cheese slices, cut into pieces
- 1/2 tsp smoked paprika
- 1/2 tsp dill weed
- 1 1/2 cups vegetable broth
- 1 tbsp almond flour
- 1/2 small onion, chopped
- 1 medium carrot, chopped
- 1 tbsp butter
- 1/2 tbsp olive oil
- Pepper
- Salt

Directions:

- Add butter into the instant pot and set pot on sauté mode.
- Once butter is melted then add onion and carrot and sauté for 2-3 minutes.
- Stir in garlic and almond flour and cook for 1 minute. Stir constantly.
- Add broth and cook for 1 minute. Add broccoli and stir well.
- Seal pot with lid and select high pressure for 8 minutes.
- Release pressure using quick release method than open the lid.
- Add paprika, dill weed, pepper, and salt.
- Add cheeses and stir until melted and combined.
- Serve hot and enjoy.

Nutritional Value (Amount per Serving):

- Calories 376
- Fat 26.2 g
- Carbohydrates 12.1 g
- Sugar 4.3 g
- Protein 22.1 g
- Cholesterol 57 mg

HEALTHY SPINACH SOUP

Time: 25 minutes

Serve: 3

Ingredients:

- 10 oz frozen spinach, thawed
- 2 tsp lemon juice
- 3 cups vegetable stock
- 1 cup cream cheese, softened
- 1 onion, chopped
- 2 tbsp butter
- Pepper
- Salt

Directions:

- Add butter into the instant pot and set the pot on sauté mode.
- Once butter is melted then add onion and sauté for 2-3 minutes.

- Add cream cheese and stir for 2 minutes. Add spinach and stir.
- Seal pot with lid and select high pressure for 3 minutes.
- Allow to release pressure naturally then open the lid.
- Stir in lemon juice and serve hot.

Nutritional Value (Amount per Serving):

- Calories 385
- Fat 37.1 g
- Carbohydrates 11 g
- Sugar 4.2 g
- Protein 9.1 g
- Cholesterol 105 mg